Quiz + Ch. 3
tonight

Second Edition

World Link

Developing English Fluency

D0128291

Soccer

Susan Stempleski
James R. Morgan
Nancy Douglas

1

Final 1,2,5,7

HEINLE
CENGAGE Learning

Australia • Brazil • Japan • Korea • Mexico • Singapore • Spain • United Kingdom • United States

HEINLE
CENGAGE Learning™

**World Link 1: Developing English Fluency
2nd Edition**

**Susan Stempleski, James R. Morgan, and
Nancy Douglas**

Publisher: Sherrise Roehr

Senior Development Editor: Jennifer Meldrum

Senior Development Editor:
  Katherine Carroll

Director of Global Marketing: Ian Martin

Senior Product Marketing Manager:
  Katie Kelley

Assistant Marketing Manager: Anders Bylund

Content Project Manager: John Sarantakis

Senior Print Buyer: Marybeth Hennebury

Composition: Pre-Press PMG

Cover/Text Design: Page2 LLC

Cover Image: iStockphoto

Library of Congress Control Number: 2009939403

ISBN-13: 978-1-4240-6818-0
ISBN-10: 1-4240-6818-5

Heinle
20 Channel Center Street
Boston, MA 02210
USA

Cengage learning is a leading provider of customized learning solutions with office locations around the globe, including Singapore, the United Kingdom, Australia, Mexico, Brazil, and Japan. Locate our local office at
www.cengage.com/global

Cengage Learning products are represented in Canada by Nelson Education, Ltd.

Visit Heinle online at **elt.heinle.com**
Visit our corporate website at **www.cengage.com**

Printed in the United States of America
2 3 4 5 6 7 15 14 13 12 11

Acknowledgments

Thank you to the educators who provided invaluable feedback throughout the development of the second edition of the *World Link* series:

Rocio Abarca, Instituto Tecnológico de Costa Rica / FUNDATEC; Anthony Acevedo, ICPNA (Instituto Cultural Peruano Norteamericano); David Aduviri, CBA (Centro Boliviano Americano) - La Paz; Ramon Aguilar, Universidad Tecnológica de Hermosillo; Miguel Arrazola, CBA (Centro Boliviano Americano) - Santa Cruz; Cecilia Avila, Universidad de Xalapa; Isabel Baracat, CCI (Centro de Comunicação Inglesa); Andrea Brotto, CEICOM (Centro de Idiomas para Comunidades); George Bozanich, Soongsil University; Emma Campo, Universidad Central; Martha Carrasco, Universidad Autonoma de Sinaloa; Herbert Chavel, Korea Advanced Institute of Science and Technology; Denise de Bartolomeo, AMICANA (Asociación Mendocina de Intercambio Cultural Argentino Norteamericano); Rodrigo de Campos Rezende, SEVEN Idiomas; John Dennis, Hokuriku University; Kirvin Andrew Dyer, Yan Ping High School; Daniela Frillochi, ARICANA (Asociación Rosarina de Intercambio Cultural Argentino Norteamericano); Jose Gonzales, ICPNA (Instituto Cultural Peruano Norteamericano); Marina Gonzalez, Instituto Universitario de Lenguas Modernas; Robert Gordon, Korea Advanced Institute of Science and Technology; Gu Yingruo, Research Institute of Xiangzhou District, ZhuHai; Yo-Tien Ho, Takming University; Roxana Jimenez, Instituto Tecnológico de Costa Rica / FUNDATEC; Sirina Kainongsuang, Perfect Publishing Company Limited; Karen Ko, ChinYi University; Ching-Hua Lin, National Taiwan University of Science and Technology; Simon Liu, ChinYi University; Maria Helena Luna, Tronwell; Ady Marrero, Alianza Cultural Uruguay Estados Unidos; Nancy Mcaleer, ELC Universidad Interamericana de Panama; Michael McCallister, Feng Chia University Language Center; José Antonio Mendes Lopes, ICBEU (Instituto Cultural Brasil Estados Unidos); Leonardo Mercado, ICPNA (Instituto Cultural Peruano Norteamericano); Tania Molina, Instituto Tecnológico de Costa Rica / FUNDATEC; Iliana Mora, Instituto Tecnológico de Costa Rica / FUNDATEC; Fernando Morales, Universidad Tecnológica de Hermosillo; Vivian Morghen, ICANA (Instituto Cultural Argentino Norteamericano); Niu Yuchun, New Oriental School Beijing; Elizabeth Ortiz, COPEI (Copol English Institute); Virginia Ortiz, Universidad Autonoma de Tamaulipas; Peter Reilly, Universidad Bonaterra; Ren Huijun, New Oriental School Hangzhou; Andreina Romero, URBE (Universidad Rafael Belloso Chacín); Adelina Ruiz, Instituto Tecnologico de Estudios Superiores de Occidente; Eleonora Salas, IICANA (Instituto de Intercambio Cultural Argentino Norteamericano); Mary Sarawit, Naresuan University International College; Jenay Seymour, Hong-ik University; Huang Shuang, Shanghai International Studies University; Sávio Siqueira, ACBEU (Asociação Cultural Brasil Estados Unidos) / UFBA (Universidade Federal da Bahia); Beatriz Solina, ARICANA (Asociación Rosarina de Intercambio Cultural Argentino Norteamericano); Tran Nguyen Hoai Chi, Vietnam USA Society English Training Service Center; Maria Inés Valsecchi, Universidad Nacional de Río Cuarto; Patricia Veciño, ICANA (Instituto Cultural Argentino Norteamericano); Punchalee Wasanasomsithi, Chulalongkorn University; Tomoe Watanabe, Hiroshima City University; Tomohiro Yanagi, Chubu University; Jia Yuan, Global IELTS School

PHOTO CREDITS:

Scope & Sequence

Unit / Lesson	Vocabulary Link	Listening	Language Link
Unit 1: New Friends, New Faces			
Lesson A Meeting new people p. 2 **Lesson B What does he look like?** p. 7	* **A web friend** p. 2 *city, e-mail address, hometown, last name* * **He's in his fifties.** p. 7 *young, tall, thin, blue eyes, long hair*	* **Where is he from?** p. 3 Make predictions Listen for details * **What does he look like?** p. 8 Use background knowledge Listen for gist and details	* **Review of the simple present** p. 5 * **Describing people:** *Be* + adjective / prepositional phrase; *Have* + (adjective) noun p. 10
Unit 2: Express Yourself!			
Lesson A What are you doing? p. 12 **Lesson B Body language and gestures** p. 17	* **A street scene** p. 12 *look (at), point (at), sit (on)* * **How do you feel?** p. 17 *excited, angry, confident*	* **Don't be nervous** p. 13 Listen for the speaker's attitude Listen for gist and details * **What are they doing?** p. 18 Infer information	* **Review of the present continuous** p. 15 * **Object pronouns** p. 20
Unit 3: What Do We Need?			
Lesson A At the supermarket p. 22 **Lesson B Let's go shopping!** p. 27	* **What's in your refrigerator?** p. 22 *chicken, fish, eggs* * **Shop or shopping?** p. 27 *shopping bag, shop online, go shopping*	* **Shopping list** p. 23 Use background knowledge Listen for details * **Going to the market** p. 28 Infer interview questions	* **Count / Noncount nouns with** *some* **and** *any* p. 25 * *Some / any, much / many, a lot of* p. 30
Review Units 1–3 p. 32			
Unit 4: Vacation!			
Lesson A How's the weather? p. 36 **Lesson B On vacation** p. 41	* **Weather words** p. 36 *rain, rainy, raining* * **When you travel** p. 41 *get a passport, go sightseeing*	* **A weather forecast** p. 37 Listen for gist and details * **On vacation** p. 42 Listen for context Dictation	* **Connecting sentences with** *but, or, so* p. 39 * *Whose;* **possessive pronouns;** *belong to* p. 4
Unit 5: Heroes			
Lesson A Risk-takers p. 46 **Lesson B Personal heroes** p. 51	* **Two people changing their world** p. 46 *traveler, researcher, explorer* * **Who is your personal hero?** p. 51 *admire, look up to, work for*	* **A dangerous job** p. 47 Use a visual cue Listen for details * **The night shift** p. 52 Listen for gist and details	* **The past tense of** *be:* **statements and** *yes / no* **questions** p. 49 * **The simple past: regular verbs and** *wh-* **questions with** *be* p. 54
Unit 6: The Mind			
Lesson A Try to remember! p. 56 **Lesson B Go back to sleep!** p. 61	* **Can you remember?** p. 56 *forget to do, good at remembering* * **Sleepwalking** p. 61 *during the day, at night, go to bed, get up*	* **There are things you can do.** p. 57 Listen for gist and details * **A nighttime story** p. 62 Listen for context Listen to sequence events	* **The simple past: irregula verbs** p. 59 * **The simple past: question forms** p. 64
Review Units 4–6 p. 66			

Pronunciation	Speaking & Speaking Strategy	Reading	Writing	Communication
Question intonation review p. 3	**Nice to meet you.** p. 4 Introducing yourself Asking about occupations	**Celebrity doubles** p. 8 Use background information and visual cues Scan for information	**Guess who?** p. 10 Describe a classmate	* **Find someone who . . .** p. 6 Ask questions to find classmates with various interests * **I'm thinking of a person.** p. 11 Ask questions to guess a mystery person
Listening for contractions p. 13	**How's it going?** p. 14 Greeting people and asking how they are	**World greetings** p. 18 Make predictions from titles and photos Scan for information	**Instant messaging** p. 21 Rewrite a text message	* **A place I know** p. 16 Draw a place your partner describes * **Act it out!** p. 21 Play a charade-style guessing game about actions
Weak vowel sounds p. 23	**We need potatoes.** p. 24 Talking about things you need	**Garage sale bargains** p. 28 Make predictions from titles and photos Identify main ideas Find synonyms	**My favorite place to shop online** p. 31 Write about a good place to shop online	* **Island survivor!** p. 26 Choose items to take on an island survival trip * **Shopping spree** p. 31 Make a list of home furnishings for a "room makeover"
Stress in compound nouns p. 37	**You should take a sweater.** p. 38 Giving advice	**A newspaper article** p. 42 Skim to choose a title Read and match numbers Read for accuracy	**Newspaper ad** p. 45 Write a want ad for a lost item	* **Where should I go?** p. 40 Choose a vacation destination for a classmate * **Are we compatible?** p. 45 Take a travel partner compatibility survey
Showing surprise p. 47	**You must really like it.** p. 48 Agreeing or disagreeing with an opinion	**Making a difference** p. 52 Scan for specific information Read for details	**My hero** p. 55 Write about a personal hero	* **Who are we going to invite?** p. 50 List famous people you want to meet and explain why * **Hero of the Year** p. 55 Choose a person to be named "Hero of the year"
The past tense -ed ending p. 57	**Maybe. I'm not sure.** p. 58 Expressing degrees of certainty	**Sleep patterns** p. 62 Use background information Identify the main point Sequence events	**Staying up late** p. 65 Write about the last time you stayed up late	* **Early memories** p. 60 Recall and share early childhood memories * **Draw and guess!** p. 65 Play a Pictionary-style game to guess about events

Scope & Sequence

Pronunciation	Speaking & Speaking Strategy	Reading	Writing	Communication
Stress in three-syllable words p. 71	**Is there a gas station near here?** p. 72 Asking for and giving directions	**The best cities** p. 76 Make predictions from titles Categorize information	**Creating a brochure** p. 79 Write an ad to promote a city	* **A death at 50 Dean Street** p. 74 Use logic to solve a crime * **Which brochure is best?** p. 79 Create and present a brochure to the class
Reduced *to* p. 81	**Do you want to play tennis?** p. 82 Inviting and offering with *Do you want...?*	**I'm a dreamer** p. 86 Use background knowledge Scan for information	**What are you like?** p. 88 Describe your personality	* **Who said that?** p. 84 Guess a classmate's identity from survey answers * **Learn about yourself** p. 89 Take a personality quiz
Contrastive stress p. 91	**Can I borrow $20?** p. 92 Making and responding to requests	**A lifetime dream** p. 96 Scan for information Find sentences to support your answers	**My dream** p. 99 Write about a future dream	* **Bad habits** p. 94 Give advice about a bad habit * **Plans for the future** p. 99 Ask and answer questions about future plans
Vowel shifts in plural forms p. 105	**I don't feel well.** p. 106 Talking about health problems	**Exam prep** p. 110 Identify the purpose for writing Choose topic sentences Infer information	**A remedy for stress** p. 113 Write about how to relieve stress	* **Health posters** p. 108 Make and present a poster to increase health awareness * **Stress survey** p. 113 Take a survey to determine your stress level
Can / can't p. 115	**You can paint really well.** p. 116 Offering compliments about things and abilities	**Two amazing achievements** p. 120 Make predictions from titles and photos Find synonyms Scan for information	**An amazing experience** p. 123 Write about an unusual personal experience	* **Talent search!** p. 118 Discover your classmates' hidden talents * **Ten things to do** p. 123 Discuss fun things to do in your lifetime
Word stress to convey meaning p. 125	**Can I take a message?** p. 126 Telephoning	**A remake** p. 130 Skim for information Categorize information	**My favorite movie** p. 133 Write about a movie you like	* **Movie reviews** p. 128 Interview a classmate about a movie * **Better the second time?** p. 133 Choose a movie to remake and decide how to do it

Language Summaries p. 138   Grammar Notes p. 144

1   Vocabulary Link   A web friend

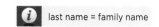
last name = family name

A   Look at Silvia's LinkBook page. Complete the website with the words in the box.

city
e-mail address
first name
~~friends~~
hometown
interests
last name
cell
languages
occupation

LinkBook » Silvia Costas

Home • Members • Inbox • Search:

LINKBOOK

See more photos
Say hello to Silvia

My _____ (3)
Dance music and hip hop, movies, traveling, learning foreign _____ (4)

World Music Awards

Travel Today!

LINKBOOK MEMBER
Silvia Costas

_____ (1)   _____ (2)

Personal Information

_____ (6):
Salvador, Brazil
Current _____ (7):
Sao Paulo
Birthdate:
Nov. 17, 1991
Relationship status:
single

Contact Information   (5)

_____ (8):
silviaC@*linkbookcom.br
_____ (9)number:
11-1212-4567

Work and school
_____ (10): **student**

Friends

Yumi

Matteo
See entire list

B   Look at Silvia's web page. Complete the questions and answers. Then practice saying them with a partner.

Saying e-mail addresses

silviaC@*linkbook.com.br =
silvia C (at) linkbook (dot) com (dot) b-r

1. _____ your name?   Silvia Costas.

2. _____ you speak English?   Yes, and I also _____ Portuguese.

3. Where are you _____ ?   I'm from Salvador.

4. _____ do you live now?   I live _____ Sao Paulo.

5. What do you _____ for fun?   I _____ to music, go to _____ , and travel.

6. _____ old are you?   I'm _____ .

In some countries, it's not polite to ask a person's age.

7. What's _____ e-mail address? It's silviaC@*linkbook.com.br.

8. What _____ you _____ ?   I'm a student.

C   Use the questions in **B** to interview each other.

2 Listening   Where is he from?

A Look at the photo of Silvia's friend from LinkBook.
Ask and answer the questions with a partner.

Where is he from?

What does he do?

What are his interests?

CD 1
Track 2

B Silvia and her friend are on her computer. Listen.
Circle the best answers.

1. His name is _____	a. Lawrence	b. Larry	c. Lars
2. He's from _____	a. Switzerland	b. England	c. Sweden
3. He speaks _____ languages.	a. two	b. three	c. four
4. He lives in _____	a. Stockholm	b. Visby	c. London
5. His hometown is _____	a. Stockholm	b. Visby	c. Bern
6. He's a _____ student.	a. business	b. mathematics	c. science
7. His interests are traveling and _____	a. music	b. languages	c. movies

C Complete sentences 1–7 in **B** about your best friend. Tell a partner about this person.

> ASK ANSWER
>
> Do you like movies? soccer? comic books? What other interests do you have?

3 Pronunciation   Question intonation review

CD 1
Track 3

A Listen to the questions. Is the intonation rising (↗) or falling (↘)?
Write arrows. Then listen again and check your answers.

1. Where is she from? ( )   3. What do they do? ( )   5. How many languages do they speak? ( )

2. Is she from Seoul? ( )   4. Do they live in Rio? ( )   6. Do you speak more than one language? ( )

CD 1
Track 4

B Listen to these conversations and repeat.

1. A: Where is she from?   2. A: What do they do?   3. A: Do you speak more than one language?

   B: She's from Korea.   B: They're artists.   B: Yes, I do.

   A: Is she from Seoul?   A: Do they live in Rio?   A: How many languages do you speak?

   B: No, she isn't.   B: Yes, they do.   B: Two—English and Spanish.

C Practice the conversations in **B** with a partner. Use your own information.

> Do you speak more than one language?
>
> Yes, I do.
>
> How many languages do you speak?
>
> Two—English and Chinese.

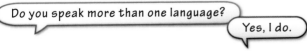

4 Speaking   Nice to meet you.

CD 1
Track 5

A   Mariana and Danny live in the same apartment building. Are they meeting for the first time? Listen to their conversation.

Mariana: Hi. My name is Mariana. I'm in apartment 201.

Danny: Hi, Mariana. I'm Danny. I'm in 302. It's nice to meet you.

Mariana: Nice to meet you, too.

Danny: So, are you a student, Mariana?

Mariana: Yeah, I study music at NYU.

Danny: That's interesting.

Mariana: What do you do, Danny?

Danny: I'm a student at Hunter College. I also work in an art gallery.

B   Practice the conversation. Then practice with *your* information.

5 Speaking Strategy

A   Introduce yourself to four classmates. Then ask about their names and occupations. Complete the chart with their information. Use the Useful Expressions to help you.

Useful Expressions	
Introducing yourself	**Asking about occupations**
A: My name is Mariana. *or* I'm Mariana.	A: What do you do?
B: (It's) Nice to meet you.	B: I'm a music student.
A: (It's) Nice to meet you, too.	

Name	Occupation(s)
Mariana	student (studies music)
1.	
2.	
3.	
4.	

B   Tell a new partner about the classmates you talked to in **A**.

> Mariana is a student. She studies music.

6 Language Link   Review of the simple present

	I/you/we/they	he/she
	speak	speaks
	study	studies
	teach	teaches
	have	has
	do	does

A Steffi is writing about herself and her classmate.
Read the sentences. Write the correct form of each verb.

Monika and Me

Monika (**1. be**)_____is_____ my classmate. We (**2. be**)_____ different in many ways. I (**3. be**)_____

an only child. Monika (**4. have**)_____ two brothers and a sister. I (**5. live**)_____ with my family.

Monika (**6. live**)_____ in her own apartment. We both go to Western University, but I (**7. study**)

_____ English Literature. Monika (**8. study**)_____ business. I (**9. not have**)_____ a job,

but Monika (**10. work**)_____ part-time at a cafe. I (**11. love**)_____ dance music, but Monika

(**12. not like**)_____ it. She (**13. listen to**)_____ rap. Monika and I (**14. watch**)_____

TV together on the weekends.

B Study the chart. Then answer the *yes/no* questions below with a partner. Use short answers.

	Yes/No **Questions**	Yes **Answers**	No **Answers**
With *be*	Are you in this class?	Yes, I am.	No, I'm not.
With other verbs	Do you speak English?	Yes, I do.	No, I don't.
With *be*	Is she in this class?	Yes, she is.	No, she isn't.
With other verbs	Does she speak English?	Yes, she does.	No, she doesn't.

1. Are Steffi and Monika different?   _____Yes, they are._____

2. Is Steffi an only child?   _____

3. Does Steffi study business?   _____

4. Do Monika and Steffi go to the same university?   _____

5. Does Monika have a job?   _____

C Read the answers below. Write the questions and then add one question of your own.
Take turns asking and answering the questions with a partner.

1. What _does Steffi study?_____   (Steffi studies) English literature.

2. Where _____   At a café.

3. Who _____   Her family.

4. Where _____   In her own apartment.

5. _____   Rap (music).

6. _____

D Think of two *yes/no* questions to ask your partner. You can ask about school, family, hobbies, job, and
favorites. For each *yes/no* question, think of a *wh*-question to ask.

E Interview your partner.

> Are you a student? Where do you go to school?

7 Communication   Find someone who . . .

A For each item in the chart, ask the question and find a person who answers *Yes*. Write his or her name. Then ask one more question and write some extra information.

Find someone who . . .	Classmate's name	Extra information
1. has a part-time job.		
2. travels sometimes.		
3. likes listening to rap music.		
4. is a university student.		
5. plays soccer.		
6. has a sister.		
7. goes to clubs on the weekends.		
8. knows his/her cell number in English.		
9. drives a car.		
10. eats breakfast every day.		
11. knows an e-mail address in English.		
12. watches movies every week.		
13. speaks three languages.		
14. is an only child.		
15.		

Do you have a part-time job?

Yes, I do.

What do you do?

I work in a coffee shop.

B Tell a classmate about the people in your chart.

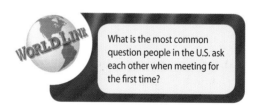

WORLD LINK

What is the most common question people in the U.S. ask each other when meeting for the first time?

New Friends, New Faces

1 Vocabulary Link   He's in his fifties.

> ⓘ teens (ages 13–19)
> twenties (ages 20–29)
> thirties forties fifties sixties

 A Complete the sentences about each person in the family photo.
Use the words in the box.

Age	Height
young	tall
in her/his twenties	average height
elderly (70+)	short

Weight	Eye color
thin	blue
slim	green
average weight	brown
heavy-set	dark

Hairstyle	Hair color
long	black
short	(light/dark) brown
straight	blond
curly	gray
spiky	red

Michael, 19
Alexis, 23
Ashley, 23
Emilio, 52
Kathy, 48

1. Emilio is _____in his fifties_____ . He is _____tall_____ . He is _____average weight_____ .
   age   height   weight
   He has _____brown_____ eyes. He has _____short_____ , _____gray_____ hair.

2. Kathy is _____ . She is _____ . She is ____thin / slim____ . She has _____
   age   height   weight
   eyes. She has _____ , straight, _____ hair.

3. Michael is _____ . He is _____ . He is _____ .
   age   height   weight
   He has _____ eyes. He has _____ , _____ , _____ hair.

4. Alexis and Ashley are _____ . They are _____ . They are _____ .
   age   height   weight
   They have _____ eyes. They have _____ , _____ , _____ hair.

 B Look again at the picture. Answer the questions with a partner.

1. Who does Michael look like?   He looks like _____his father_____ .
2. Who does Ashley look like?   She looks like _____ . They're twins.
3. Who do you look like?   I look like _____ .

 C Describe a friend or a family member to a partner.
Use the sentences in **A** to help you.

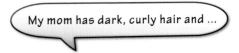
> My mom has dark, curly hair and …

2 Listening What does he look like?

 A Look at the pictures below. Describe the man's appearance in each one.

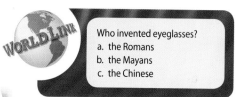

WORLD LINK

Who invented eyeglasses?
a. the Romans
b. the Mayans
c. the Chinese

a.

b.

c.

 B Listen and answer the question.

CD 1
Track 6

Why is Emily at the airport?
- ☐ 1. She's buying souvenirs.
- ☐ 2. She's meeting her uncle.
- ☐ 3. She's traveling to another country.

 C Circle the words that describe Uncle Tim. Then check the picture of Uncle Tim in **A**.

CD 1
Track 7

1. Uncle Tim <u>before</u>:

short / tall   short hair / long hair   brown hair / blond hair

2. Uncle Tim <u>now</u>:

short / tall   short hair / long hair   brown hair / blond hair

3 Reading Celebrity doubles

A Look at the photo on page 9. Who is it? What do you know about him?

B Read the first two paragraphs. Circle *True* or *False*.

1. Andrew Walker is English.	True	False
2. He's an actor.	True	False
3. People stop him on the street.	True	False
4. He looks like a famous pop star.	True	False

Celebrity
Doubles

A group of teenagers is standing outside a shop in Manchester, England. Many of them have cameras and are looking in the shop window. They want to see movie star Daniel Radcliffe. A man in the shop looks like Radcliffe (he has brown hair and Radcliffe's good looks). But the young man in the shop isn't the famous actor. He's Andrew Walker — a twenty-two-year-old shop clerk.

Walker isn't surprised by the teenagers. People often stop him on the street and want to take his picture. Walker is a clerk, but he also makes money as Daniel's double. Walker travels all over Europe as Daniel Radcliffe. Newspapers often take his photo. It's an exciting life for the shop clerk from Manchester.

Today, many companies work with celebrity doubles. The most popular celebrity doubles look like famous athletes, pop singers, and actors. The companies pay doubles to go to parties and business meetings. Doubles are also on TV and in newspaper ads.

Why do people want to look like a celebrity? One double in the U.S. says, "I can make good money. I also make a lot of people happy."

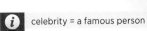

ⓘ celebrity = a famous person

C Complete the chart.

	Andrew Walker	celebrity doubles
Who do they look like?		
How do they make money?		

ASK ANSWER

Who are popular celebrities in your country? What are they famous for?
Imagine you can invite a celebrity double to a class party. Who do you want to invite? Why?

4 Language Link   Describing people

A Complete the sentences below with the correct form of *be* or *have*. Use the chart to help you.

What does she look like?	
be + adjective/prepositional phrase	*have* + (adjective) noun
Christina is tall and slim.	Mayumi has brown eyes and straight, black hair.
She's in her twenties. She's young.	

1. Ricardo _____has_____ curly hair.
2. Monique _____ in her eighties. She _____ elderly.
3. I _____ blue eyes.
4. Max and Charlie are twins. Max _____ a beard and a mustache. Charlie _____ clean-shaven. They both _____ blond hair.
5. Tanya's dad _____ average height.
6. Damon _____ heavy. He weighs about 136 kilos!

B Look at the photo of Usain Bolt and make sentences about him. Describe his appearance.

1. HAIR: He has _____ hair.
2. EYES: _____ .
3. AGE: _____ . He's young.
4. HEIGHT: _____ .
5. WEIGHT: He's _____ weight.
6. NATIONALITY: He's _____ .

> Usain Bolt

 C Describe a beautiful woman or handsome man. This can be a real person or not a real person. Tell your partner what he or she looks like. Your partner can ask questions.

5 Writing   Guess who?

 A Read the paragraph on the right. Then write five or six sentences about a classmate. Don't write your classmate's name.

B Exchange your writing with a partner. Guess the person.

My classmate is in his twenties. He's average height—he's about 172 centimeters. He has short, straight, brown hair. He has dark brown eyes (I think). He's clean-shaven, and he wears glasses.

6 Communication **I'm thinking of a person.**

A Look at the photo on the right. With your partner, say one sentence each that describes the woman.

She has blue eyes.

She's slim.

B Now practice this conversation.
Do you understand the guessing game?

GUESSING GAME

Student A: I'm thinking of a person.

Student B: Is the person a man?

A: No, she isn't.

B: Is she tall?

A: Yes, she is.

B: Does she have dark hair?

A: No, she doesn't.

B: Is she young?

A: Yes, sort of.

B: Well, is she in her thirties?

A: No, she's not.

B: Is she in her twenties?

A: Yes, I think so.

C Think of a famous person. Your partner asks questions and guesses the person. Then switch roles.

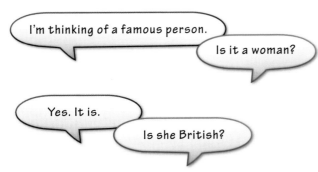

I'm thinking of a famous person.

Is it a woman?

Yes. It is.

Is she British?

 Check out the World Link video.   Practice your English online at http://elt.heinle.com/worldlink

1   Vocabulary Link   A street scene

bark
look
point
shout
sit
smile
talk
wave

A   Look at the picture above. What are the people doing? Complete the sentences.
Use the correct form of the verbs in the box. Notice the words in blue.

1. She's _____talking_____ to her friend.
2. She's _____smiling_____ at her friend.
3. He's _____looking_____ at the two women.
4. She's _____waving_____ to her family.
5. She's _____pointing_____ at the man.
6. She's _____sitting_____ on the bench.
7. It's _____barking_____ at the girl.
8. He's _____shouting_____ at the driver.

B   Choose a person in the picture. Tell a story about the person.

> She's talking to her friend.
> Maybe they're going to the movies.

2 Listening Don't be nervous

A What makes you happy or sad? What makes you relaxed or nervous?

nervous

sad

happy

relaxed

CD 1
Track 8

B Listen to three conversations. Number the pictures 1, 2, or 3 in the order you hear them.

3

1

2

CD 1
Track 8

C Listen again. How does each speaker feel? Circle the correct adjective.
Then complete the sentences with the correct words.

1. Angie is relaxed / (nervous.)   Reason: She has an important _exam_ .

2. Carolyn is happy / (sad.)   Reason: Her boyfriend is _traviing._

3. (Vicki is happy) / sad.   Reason: They can't find a _hotel_ . Now she can go to _London_

3 Pronunciation Listening for contractions

CD 1
Track 9

A Listen to the sentences. Notice the pronunciation of the underlined words.

1. It's summer vacation and you're leaving!

2. I'm talking to you!

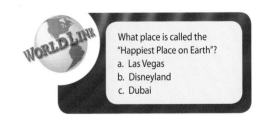

WORLD LINK

What place is called the "Happiest Place on Earth"?
a. Las Vegas
b. Disneyland
c. Dubai

CD 1
Track 10

B Listen and circle the choices you hear.

1. What is / What's the capital of Greenland?

2. Why is / Why's she laughing?

3. I am / I'm planning our trip to Las Vegas.

4. It is / It's a cool website.

C Practice saying the sentences in **A** and **B** with a partner.

4 Speaking **How's it going?**

A Read the conversation and listen. How is Katy? Explain your answer to a partner.

Jim: Hi, Katy.

Katy: Hey, Jim. How's it going?

Jim: Great! How're you doing?

Katy: So-so.

Jim: Yeah? What's wrong?

Katy: Oh, I have an important test tomorrow.

Jim: But you're not studying.

Katy: Well, I'm kind of tired.

Jim: Why don't you take a break and drink some coffee? We can go to a cafe together.

Katy: And then I can study later. Sounds good!

B Practice the conversation with a partner. Then ask your partner how he or she is today.

5 Speaking Strategy

A Read the two situations below. Write two new conversations on a separate sheet of paper. Use the conversation in **A** and the Useful Expressions to help you.

> **Situation 1**
>
> **Student A:** You're stressed. You have two tickets to a basketball game tonight. You're going with your friend, but your friend is late.
> **Student B:** Your suggestion: Take a taxi to the game. Maybe the friend is there.

> **Situation 2**
>
> **Student A:** You're unhappy. You live in New York. Your cousin lives in Boston. She wants you to visit her. Plane tickets are expensive right now.
> **Student B:** Your suggestion: Rent a car and drive from New York to Boston.

> ### Useful Expressions
>
> **Greeting people and asking how they are**
>
> A: Hi, _____ . How's it going?/
> Hi, _____ . How're you doing?
>
> B: Fine. / OK. / All right. / Pretty good./
> Not bad. How about you?
>
> A: I'm fine.
>
> :(A: Hi, _____ . How's it going?/
> Hi, _____ . How're you doing?
>
> B: So-so. / Not so good.
>
> A: Really? What's wrong?
>
> B: I have a big test tomorrow.
> I'm (a little) stressed.
> I'm (kind of) tired.
>
> *I'm stressed* = I feel nervous
> *kind of* = a little

B Role play one conversation for another pair.

6 Language Link Review of the present continuous

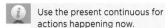
Use the present continuous for actions happening now.

subject + *am* / *is* / *are* + verb *-ing*

A What are the neighbors doing? Write sentences. Use the present continuous.

1. They are sitting on a sofa.
2. They're
3.
4.

5.
6.
7.
8.

B Think of questions to ask about the picture. Take turns asking and answering the questions with a partner.

1. What *are thay drinking?*
2. Why *thay are exiting?*
3. Who *is she?*
4. *who is angry?*

> What are the two people talking about?
>
> Maybe they're talking about music.

C Take turns making true sentences with the present continuous. Use the words below. Then make one sentence of your own.

1. I / wear / glasses *I wearin a sunglasses in the morning.*
2. I / eat / lunch *I eated my lunch today*
3. My classmates / sit on / chairs *My classmate sites on his chair.*
4. It / rain *it is raing raight now.*
5. We / speak / English *we are speaking english right now*
6. Our teacher / talk *6. our teacher is talkative.*

7 Communication   A place I know

A Think of a place in your city or a famous place in the world. Write it down. (Don't show anyone!)

_____

B Imagine you are in the place you wrote down in **A.**
What are people doing? What do you see? Write four or five
sentences about your place. See the example for ideas.

Example: *It's a beautiful city. There is a lot of water. Two people are riding in
a boat. A man is standing in the boat. He is pushing. They are going
under a bridge.*

_____

_____

_____

_____

C Do the following:

Student A: Read your sentences to a partner.

Student B: Draw the place your partner describes in the box below.

Student A: Check your partner's drawing. Is it accurate? Can your partner guess the place?

D Switch roles and do **C** again.

Express Yourself!

1 Vocabulary Link How do you feel?

A Complete the chart with the words in the box. Are any of these words opposites?

> I'M. . .   confused   angry   cold   bored

1. _____
2. _____
3. _____
4. _____
5. confident

6. embarrassed
7. excited
8. hot
9. hungry
10. thirsty

B Complete the sentences below with an adjective from **A**.

1. I'm _____ . Can you open the window?

2. He's always studying. I'm _____ that he'll do well on the exam.

3. I think the teacher is _____ . She's shouting at a student.

4. I have a big hole in my pants. I'm so _____ .

5. Can I have that sweater? I'm _____ .

6. I'm so _____ ! We're leaving for Hawaii today!

7. I'm _____ with this show. There's nothing good on TV tonight.

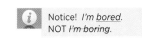 Notice! *I'm bored*.
NOT *I'm boring*.

C Answer the questions below. Use a word in **A** or another word you know.

How do you feel...
> in the morning?   when you speak English?   right now?
> before a big exam?   about summer vacation?

D Ask and answer the questions with a partner.

> How do you feel right now?

> I'm hungry! What time is lunch?

2 Listening   What are they doing?

A Study these gestures. Complete the sentences with the expressions in the box. Do these gestures have the same meaning in your country?

> call someone   cross your fingers   point to something   shrug your shoulders

You can _____
to say "I don't know."

You can _____
for good luck.

You can say "Come here"
by using your
hand to _____ .

You can _____
by using only one finger.

B Listen to four conversations. Match the gesture in **A** that you think is used in each conversation.

CD 1
Track 12

1. ☐   2. ☐   3. ☐   4. ☐

C Listen again. Complete each sentence with the correct answer.

CD 1
Track 12

rushed = in a hurry

1. Paula is rushed / relaxed.

2. The man is excited / bored.

3. Anne is nervous / confident about her exam.

4. Bill is confident / confused.

3 Reading   World greetings

A Look at the title and photos on p. 19. Complete the definition.

> A <u>greeting</u> is a way to say _____ .

What are some things people say and do when they meet someone for the first time?

B Where do people use these greetings? Scan the reading on p. 19 and check (✔) your answers.

	Brazil	New Zealand	Japan
1. bow	☐	☐	☑
2. kiss	☐	☐	☐
3. press noses together	☐	☐	☐
4. shake hands	☐	☐	☐

WorldView

World Greetings

kiss on the cheek

Brazil
Men often shake hands when they meet for the first time. When women meet, they kiss each other on the cheek. Women also kiss male friends to say hello.

When you shake hands, look the person in the eyes. This shows interest and friendliness.

New Zealand
Usually, both men and women shake hands when they meet someone for the first time.

Fun fact: If you see two people pressing their noses together, they are probably Maori. The Maori are the native people of New Zealand. This is their traditional greeting.

Japan
When people meet for the first time, they usually bow. In business, people also shake hands.

In formal situations, people often exchange business cards. When you give a business card, give it with two hands. This is polite.

Special note: In Japan, a smile can have different meanings. It usually means that the person is happy, or that the person thinks something is funny. But it can also mean that the person is embarrassed.

shake hands

press noses together

bow

C These sentences are false. Read the article. Make them true. Tell a partner.

1. In Brazil, women kiss other women as a greeting. Women don't kiss men.
2. When you shake hands, don't look the person in the eyes.
3. In Japan, you give a business card with one hand.
4. In Japan, a smile always means you are happy.

D In each situation below, what greeting do you use? What do you say?

you see a friend in a cafe

you meet your teacher on the street

you interview for a job with Mr. Jones

you see your boy/girlfriend after class

4 Language Link   Object pronouns

A Complete the sentences below with the correct subject and object pronouns. Use the information in the box to help you.

1. *subject* *object*
   David kisses his mother every day.
   ___He___ kisses ___her___ every day.

2. Mrs. Wang is yelling at Carlos.
   _____ is shouting at _____ .

3. The dog is barking at Simone and me.
   _____ is barking at _____ .

4. Simone and I are nervous about the test.
   _____ are nervous about _____ .

5. In Japan, people give their business cards with two hands. In Japan, _____ give _____ with two hands.

6. I am waving to you and Leo. I am waving to _____ . Can you see _____ ?

Pronouns	
Subject Pronouns	**Object Pronouns**
I	me
you	you
he	him
she	her
it	it
we	us
you (pl)	you
they	them

B Read the sentences. Circle the subject. Underline the object.

1. (Angie) is waving to her son.
2. Tom is smiling at Jane.
3. Carlos is worried about the test.
4. Do your parents like Indian food?
5. Peter and Cindy are talking to Bill and Anna.
6. Rick and I can meet you and Mike at 3:00.
7. The dog is barking at Taylor and me.
8. Maya is calling Beth on her cell phone.

C Rewrite the sentences in **B**. Use the correct subject and object pronouns.

1. *She's waving to him.* _____
2. _____
3. _____
4. _____
5. _____
6. _____
7. _____
8. _____

D Complete the sentences. Which ones are true for you? Tell a partner.

1. English class is difficult, but I like _____ a lot.
2. I speak English at school and I use _____ at home, too.
3. My parents listen to _____ and I listen to _____ .
4. _____ is my best friend and I talk _____ every day.
5. _____ is our English teacher and I see _____ every day at school.

5 Writing Instant messaging

A Koji and Paloma are classmates. They're instant messaging. Match the underlined expressions with their meanings in the box.

Paloma:	hi koji
Koji:	hey. how <u>r u</u>
Paloma:	<u>Gr8!</u> and you
Koji:	good. a little bored. not studying.
Paloma:	I know the feeling
Koji:	<u>r u</u> ready for the test?
Paloma:	no, but meeting Jennie <u>f2f</u> tomorrow to study. you can come too
Koji:	<u>thx</u>
Palmoa:	I'll call you tomorrow.
Koji:	<u>K</u>
Palmoa:	<u>ttyl</u>
Koji:	<u>c u later</u>

are you

face to face

great

how are you

okay

see you later

talk to you later

thanks

B Rewrite the conversation in **A** in full sentences. Add any missing words. Use correct punctuation.

C Compare your answers with a partner.

Hi, Koji.

Hey. How are you?

Great! And you?

Good. I'm a little bored.

I'm not…

6 Communication Act it out!

Get into a group of three people. Read the directions to play this game.

Student A: Choose a sentence below. Act out the sentences for Students B and C. Do *not* use words.

Students B and C: Watch Student A. Be the first to say the sentence Student A is doing. If you guess correctly, you get a point. Play until all sentences are done.

I'm hungry.	Relax!	Look at that!	I'm nervous.
This is delicious.	Good luck!	Come here!	This tastes terrible.
Stop it!	Really? That's surprising!	I'm bored.	I'm not listening!
Let's go!	Go away!	I'm angry.	Sit down.
Be quiet.	Peace.	What? I can't hear you.	See you later.
I'm sad.	You have a phone call.	He's crazy.	I'm not sure.

 Check out the World Link video. Practice your English online at http://elt.heinle.com/worldlink

3 What Do We Need?
Lesson A At the supermarket

1 Vocabulary Link   What's in your refrigerator?

describing *food*
fast	junk
fresh	organic
frozen	prepared

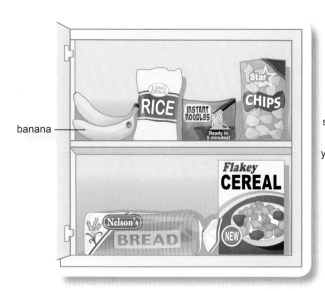

banana

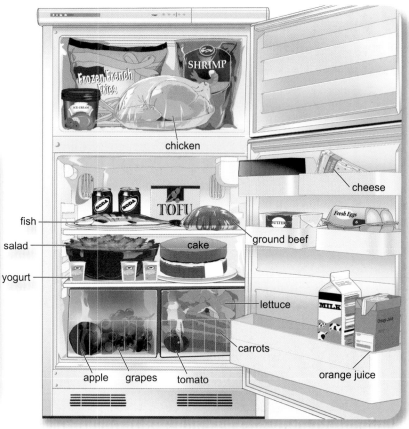

chicken

cheese

fish

ground beef

salad

cake

yogurt

lettuce

carrots

apple grapes tomato

orange juice

A Study the picture for 20 seconds. Then close your book. Say the food and drinks you remember.

B Which foods and drinks in the photo are good for you?
Which aren't? Complete the chart. Compare answers with a partner.

good for you	not good for you

Fish is *good* for you. But frozen French fries aren't! They're junk food.

C Ask and answer the questions with a partner.

1. Which things in **A** do you eat or drink often? sometimes? never?

2. Do you eat a lot of fast food or junk food (chips, candy, soda)?

3. Do you usually eat fresh food or prepared food?

2 Listening   Shopping list

> Where do you usually buy your food?   What do you buy there?

A Look at the two pictures below. What's in each bag? Make two lists.

B Listen. Which shopping bag is Allison's? Circle it.

CD 1
Track 13

CD 1
Track 14

C Listen. Allison's mom changes one item on the list. Put an X on the item in the shopping bag. Write the name of the new item.

CD 1
Track 15

D How do Allison and her mom talk about the foods they need? Do you remember? Complete the sentences with the words in the box. Then listen and check your answers.

> bunch   carton   head   loaf

1. I need a _____ of bread.

2. and a _____ of lettuce

3. a _____ of ice cream

4. Please get a _____ of carrots, OK?

3 Pronunciation   Weak vowel sounds

CD 1
Track 16

A Listen to the words. Notice the stressed syllables in BLUE and the unstressed vowels (/ə/).

baNAna = bənanə   CARrot = carrət   KETCHup = ketchəp

> _i_ In unstressed syllables, the vowel sound is reduced. The schwa /ə/ is the symbol for these vowels.

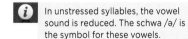
CD 1
Track 17

B Listen and say the words. Put a line [\] through the unstressed, reduced vowels.

chicken   vanilla   vitamin

soda   potato   lettuce

orange   bandage   pizza

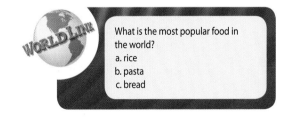

What is the most popular food in the world?
a. rice
b. pasta
c. bread

4 Speaking **We need potatoes.**

CD 1
Track 18

A Read the conversation and listen. Underline the foods Ken and Rachel have. Circle the foods they need.

Ken: Rachel, I'm making a shopping list for our barbecue. We have chicken. What else do we need?

Rachel: Let's see . . . we need some potatoes.

Ken: Okay, got it.

Rachel: We also need lettuce and tomatoes for the salad.

Ken: And what about drinks? Do we need any?

Rachel: Let's see . . . We have soda.

Ken: Okay. I'll buy some juice then. See you!

B Practice the conversation with a partner. Then make your own conversation. Use your own ideas for the words in blue.

5 Speaking Strategy

A Imagine you are having a class party. Everyone in class must bring something to the party. Think of an idea and write it on the board.

B Look at the checklist below. These are things you need for the party. Look at the items on the board. Use the Useful Expressions to talk about the things you have and the things you need for your party.

Class party checklist

food

drinks

dessert

napkins, cups, plates

forks, spoons, knives, chopsticks, etc.

chairs

other (add your ideas):

Useful Expressions
Talking about things you need

Do we need any drinks?
　Yes, we need soda and bottled water.
　Yes, we do. We need. . .
　No, we don't. We (already) have drinks.

What else do we need?
　We still need. . .
　Nothing. I think we're all set.

Anything else?
　Yes, we need. . .
　No, that's it. We have everything.

C Share your ideas in **B** with another pair.

6 Language Link   Count / Noncount nouns with *some* and *any*

A   Study the chart. Then complete each sentence with "C" (for count nouns) or "N" (for noncount nouns).

1. _____ can follow *a* or *an*.

2. _____ can follow numbers (*one, two,* etc.)

3. _____ are always singular.

4. _____ have a singular and plural form.

noncount nouns	count nouns
bread	a tomato
coffee	an orange
sand	two books
food	three grapes

B   Complete the sentences with *a, an,* or nothing.

1. Do you want _____ rice or _____ baked potato with your dinner?

2. Billy wants _____ fruit. Give him _____ apple.

3. Do you usually put _____ sugar in _____ tea?

4. I often read _____ magazine on the train to school.

5. Is there _____ salt in this soup?

6. I eat _____ egg and _____ banana for breakfast.

C   Study the chart. Then complete the conversation about a dinner party with *some* or *any*.

	Question	Positive answer	Negative answer
Noncount nouns	Do we have any lettuce?	Yes, we have some (lettuce).	No, we don't have any (lettuce).
Plural count nouns	Do we have any potatoes?	Yes, we have some (potatoes). Yes, we have three (potatoes).	No, we don't have any (potatoes).

Alberto: I'm excited about tonight. Listen, do you need (1) _____ help?

Lucia: Actually, yes. Can you make the salad?

Alberto: Sure! But first, do you have (2) _____ soap?

Lucia: Yeah, there's (3) _____ next to the sink.

Alberto: Thanks. Now, let's see . . . do you have (4) _____ lettuce?

Lucia: Yes, there's (5) _____ in the refrigerator.

Alberto: Great. Is there (6) _____ yogurt for the dressing?

Lucia: No, I don't have (7) _____ .

Alberto: OK. I'll go to the store and buy (8) _____ now.

   D   Practice the conversation with your partner.

7 Communication   Island survivor!

A   Read about this TV show.

There is a new reality show on TV. On this show, people stay on an island for one month to win money. Here is some information about the island:

- It's in the Pacific Ocean.
- In the afternoon, it's very hot—100 degrees F / 38 degrees C.
- There's very little drinking water on the island.
- There are some fruit trees on the island.

You want to be on this TV show. For your stay on the island, you can choose six items from the list below. Is there anything you want to add to the list? Write it. Then circle the six items you need.

meat	toothpaste	bananas	bandages	knife
bottled water	soap	oranges	coffee or tea	matches
rice	sunscreen	magazines	toilet paper	_____
bread	hat	shampoo	vitamins	_____

 B   Join a group of three to four people. Compare your answers. Explain your choices. Together make *one* list of six items.

 C   Explain your final list to the class.

> We need some bottled water. There's very little drinking water on the island.

What Do We Need?

Lesson B   Let's go shopping!

1   Vocabulary Link   **Shop or shopping?**

A   Read the questions and responses. Complete the sentences with the words *shop(s)* or *shopping*.

> I _____shop_____ at Nancy's. [verb]   I like _____shopping_____. [noun]
> It's a nice _____shop_____. [noun]   There's a new _____shopping_____ center. [adjective]

Who does the (1) grocery _____shopping_____ in your home?

My mother. My sister likes to help. She pushes the (2) _____ cart. Me? I don't like to (3) go _____ at all.

Where's your favorite place to shop?

The (6) _____ mall. It's great because you can (7) _____ around for the best prices. My friends and I also like to go (8) window _____.

My husband. He buys the food. He brings his own (4) _____ bag to the store. It's good for the Earth! Me? I do a lot of (5) _____ online. It's fast and easy.

There's a great bookstore in my neighborhood. You can spend hours there! On the top floor, there's also a (9) gift _____. There's a (10) coffee _____, too.

B   Ask and answer the questions in **A**. Then tell your partner your answers to the questions below.

Do you like grocery shopping? window shopping? online shopping? Why or why not?

ASK   ANSWER

What other kinds of shops do you know?

2 Listening **Going to the market**

Look at the three photos below. Tell your partner the things you see in the photos. What do they sell at the different markets?

A Jonathan works in a market. Which one is it? Listen. Circle your answer.

CD 1
Track 19

produce market

fish market

flower market

B Listen again. You will only hear Jonathan's responses.
Match each response with the question Jonathan was asked.

CD 1
Track 19

1. response #1
2. response #2
3. response #3
4. response #4

a. What do you sell?
b. What's special about your market?
c. Is it busy?
d. Do you like your work?

ASK ANSWER

Which market is interesting to you? Why? Is there a market like this in your city? What can you buy there?

C Listen again. Circle the correct answers. (In some cases, two answers are possible.)

CD 1
Track 19

1. The market is busy before 5 a.m. / 8 a.m.
2. You can buy items from Thailand / Holland.

3. The market has nice smells / colors.
4. You can buy flowers online / in the coffee shop.

3 Reading **Garage sale bargains**

Look at the title of the reading and the photo on the next page. What do you think a garage sale is?

A Answer the question. Explain your answer to your partner.
What do you do with your old clothes, furniture, books, bikes, or TVs?

☐ I sell them.

☐ I give them to friends and family.

☐ I put them in the garbage.

☐ I keep them for a long time.

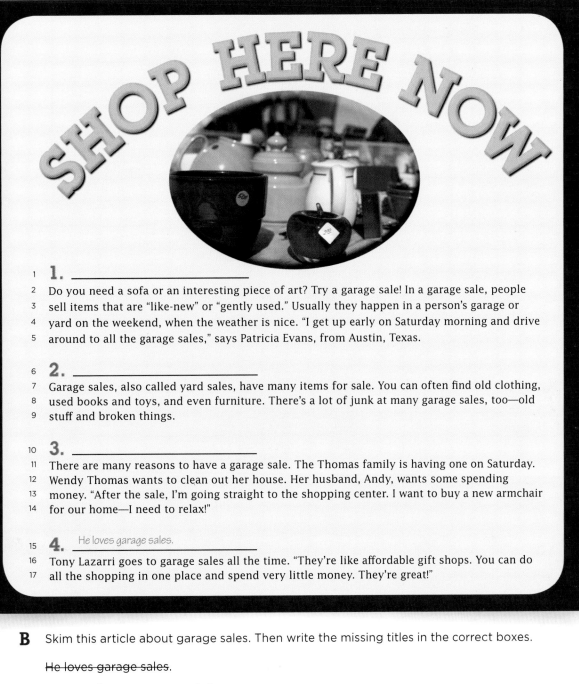

SHOP HERE NOW

1. 1. _____
2. Do you need a sofa or an interesting piece of art? Try a garage sale! In a garage sale, people
3. sell items that are "like-new" or "gently used." Usually they happen in a person's garage or
4. yard on the weekend, when the weather is nice. "I get up early on Saturday morning and drive
5. around to all the garage sales," says Patricia Evans, from Austin, Texas.

6. 2. _____
7. Garage sales, also called yard sales, have many items for sale. You can often find old clothing,
8. used books and toys, and even furniture. There's a lot of junk at many garage sales, too—old
9. stuff and broken things.

10. 3. _____
11. There are many reasons to have a garage sale. The Thomas family is having one on Saturday.
12. Wendy Thomas wants to clean out her house. Her husband, Andy, wants some spending
13. money. "After the sale, I'm going straight to the shopping center. I want to buy a new armchair
14. for our home—I need to relax!"

15. 4. *He loves garage sales.* _____
16. Tony Lazarri goes to garage sales all the time. "They're like affordable gift shops. You can do
17. all the shopping in one place and spend very little money. They're great!"

B Skim this article about garage sales. Then write the missing titles in the correct boxes.

~~He loves garage sales.~~

I want to have a garage sale because. . .

Things at a garage sale

What is a garage sale?

C For items 1–3, circle the correct answers. For items 4–6, write words with the same meaning.

1. In line 16, *affordable* means expensive / not expensive.

2. In line 8, *junk* means useless / useful things.

3. In lines 12–13, *spending money* means extra money for necessary / unnecessary items.

4. In paragraph 2, this is another word for *garage sales*. _____

5. In paragraph 3, this is another word for *shopping mall*. _____

6. In paragraph 4, this is another word for *souvenir shops*. _____

4 Language Link *Some / any, much / many, a lot of*

A With a partner, look at the picture below and complete the sentences in the chart. Use the words in the box.

| ~~shoes~~ | clothing | furniture | toys | hats |

	Noncount nouns			Count nouns		
Positive	There's	a lot of _____.		There are	a lot of *shoes* .	
		some	jewelry.		some _____.	
Negative	There isn't	much	_____.	There aren't	many	books.
		any	software.		any	_____.

Garage Sale Today!

B Complete the sentences with *some, any, much, many,* or *a lot of.*

1. John won $1,000,000 in the lottery! Now he has _____*a lot of*_____ money.

2. Barry only has $5 in his bank account. He doesn't have _____ money.

3. Rita has _____ beautiful jade jewelry: two bracelets and a pair of earrings.

4. Carla is an only child. She doesn't have _____ brothers or sisters.

5. Leo is really popular. He has _____ friends.

6. I don't have _____ friends—just two from college. But, we're very close.

5 Writing   My favorite place to shop online

A Read about this person's favorite place to shop online. Then write about your favorite place.

- What's the name of the website?
- What can you buy there?
- Why do you like it?

 B Exchange your writing with a partner. Ask your partner one question about his or her favorite place.

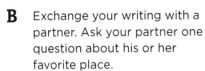

I like to shop online at Moby's Music. They sell all kinds of music—pop, rock, hip hop, and my favorite, world music. You can find a lot of music at a great price! I download songs and then burn CDs for my friends. My friends love their gifts!

6 Communication   Shopping spree

 A Read about Jessie. Then describe her apartment with a partner.

Jessie is a 22-year-old university exchange student. She's living in your country for one year. She lives in a small apartment near her school. This is her apartment.

> There isn't much furniture in the apartment.

 B Jessie's parents live in the United States. They want to visit her. Help Jessie prepare for her parents' visit.

- What does her apartment have?
- What does her apartment need? Make a list.
- Where can she buy the things? Put your ideas on the list.

Things Jessie needs	Place to shop

> She needs some chairs in the kitchen. She can buy them at Daisy's Department Store.

 C Compare your list with another pair's list.

 Check out the World Link video.   Practice your English online at http://elt.heinle.com/worldlink

1 Storyboard

 A Lisa and Eva are roommates. Look at the pictures and work with a partner to complete the conversations. More than one answer is possible for most blanks.

 B Practice the conversation with a partner. Then change roles and practice again.

2 See It and Say It

A Describe a person in the picture below to your partner. Don't say the person's name. Your partner guesses the person.

B Talk about the picture.

- Where are these people?
- What are they doing?
- Which people are meeting for the first time? How do you know?
- Ask one question about the picture.

> This person is tall. The person has long hair and . . .

C Choose one pair or group of people. With a partner, role play a conversation of five to six sentences between the people.

> Hi, I'm Felipe . . .

> Hi, Felipe. Nice to meet you. My name is . . .

3 Odd Word Out

A Look at the words. Circle the one that is different in each group.

1. nervous	embarrassed	angry	happy
2. grape	carrot	corn	lettuce
3. red	gray	curly	black
4. cheese	yogurt	milk	orange juice
5. heavy-set	short	slim	thin
6. point at	bark at	wave to	talk to
7. shopper	shopping cart	shopping bag	shopping mall

B Compare and explain your answers with a partner.

> For number 1, happy is different. It's a good feeling. Nervous, embarrassed, and angry are bad feelings.

4 Do You Ever . . . ?

A Read each question. Answer *Yes* or *No*. Then write a sentence to give some extra information. Use the correct pronouns in your answers.

1. Do <u>you</u> give <u>your mom</u> flowers?

   Yes. I give her flowers on her birthday.

2. Does <u>your mom</u> speak to <u>your dad</u> in English?

   _____

3. Do <u>you</u> take <u>the bus</u> to school?

   _____

4. Do <u>your friends</u> send <u>you</u> text messages?

   _____

5. Does <u>your teacher</u> give <u>your class</u> homework?

   _____

6. Do <u>you and your friends</u> give <u>your homework</u> to your teacher late?

   _____

B Ask your partner the questions in **A**. Listen to his or her answers. Then, ask your partner one more question.

5 Listening: The Perfect Diet?

A Tino and Mary are talking about Tino's diet. Listen and circle your answers.

CD 1
Track 20

1. Which sentence is true?

    a. Mary thinks Tino eats too much.
    b. Tino is worried about his health.
    c. Mary thinks Tino's diet is too unhealthy.
    d. Tino is worried about Mary's health.

2. What is Tino NOT eating?

    a. protein
    b. vegetables
    c. fruit

B Listen again. Which foods can he eat? Check the boxes.

CD 1
Track 20

C Discuss this question with a partner and explain your opinion: Is Tino's diet healthy?

6 Talk About . . .

A Get into a group of three people and do this activity.

1. One person chooses a topic from the list and says it to the group.

2. Each person in the group asks the first person a question about the topic.
   That person answers each question.

3. Take turns and repeat steps 1 and 2 for each topic.

   - your hobbies
   - why you are learning English
   - your favorite music
   - a country you want to visit

   - your favorite TV show
   - your favorite food
   - your best friend
   - something you don't like

1 Vocabulary Link Weather words

A Look at this chart of weather words. Fill in the missing words.

	noun	adjective	*It + -ing* verb
	sun		
		cloudy	
	rain*		raining
	snow*		
		windy	
	fog		

We often use a form of *be* with these weather words:
The sun is bright.
It's foggy today.

*However, you can use *snow* and *rain* as verbs without *be*:
It snows/rains a lot here.

B Josh is talking about the weather where he lives. Complete the sentences with the correct form of each word. Compare your answers with a partner. Is the weather similar where you live?

a breeze = a light wind

In December and January, many mornings are

_____ . Most of our _____ falls in
(fog)   (snow)
February. In fact, it's _____ here right now!
            (snow)

Spring is usually cool and wet. When it's _____
          (rain)
like this for days and days, I feel depressed.

I look forward to summer. The days are hot and _____ ,
              (sun)
while the nights are cool and _____ .
        (breeze)

The weather changes almost every day. Strong _____
              (wind)
can bring a lot of _____ .
      (rain)
Partly _____ days are common.
    (cloud)

hot

warm

chilly

cold

freezing

C Imagine someone wants to visit your city or country. Can you tell them about the weather?

Summers in Buenos Aires are hot and dry.

2 Listening A weather forecast

A How do you get your weather information—from the TV, radio, or Internet?
Do you trust weather forecasts? Discuss with a partner.

CD 1
Track 21

B In general, how is the weather going to be on Friday, Saturday, and Sunday?
Listen and match a picture (A, B, C) with the correct day(s). One picture is extra.

Friday: _____

Saturday: _____

Sunday: _____

> **ⓘ Word partnerships**
> heavy / light rain
> strong / light winds
> clear / (partly) cloudy skies
> cool / warm temperatures

CD 1
Track 21

C How is the weather going to be during the day and in the evening on each day?
Listen again. Complete the chart with words from the box.

| clear | cloudy | cool | rainy | sunny | warm | windy |

Friday, June 19		Saturday, June 20		Sunday, June 21	
a.m.	**p.m.**	**a.m.**	**p.m.**	**a.m.**	**p.m.**
	clear	sunny			rainy
warm				cool	

D Tell a partner about the weather on Friday, Saturday, and Sunday.

> On Friday, it's going to be sunny and warm. In the evening . . .

3 Pronunciation Stress in compound nouns

CD 1
Track 22

A Listen to these sentences. Notice the stress of the underlined words.

Where are my **sun**glasses?   What's today's **fore**cast?

CD 1
Track 23

B Listen to these sentences. What do you notice about the word stress of the underlined words? Practice saying these sentences with a partner.

1. Let's look at the weather map.
2. Don't forget your raincoat!

3. Many people wear sunscreen at the beach.
4. Tomorrow we'll see lots of sunshine.

> **WORLD LINK**
> How often does lightning strike the Earth?
> a. a thousand times every second
> b. a hundred times every second
> c. a thousand times every minute

4 Speaking   **You should take a sweater.**

CD 1
Track 24

A   Read the conversation and listen. Then complete the conversation with the words in the box.

foggy	Los Angeles	pants	San Francisco	shorts	warm

Kyle: There! All finished!

Juliet: Wait a minute. . . You're going to San Francisco, right?

Kyle: Yeah. See? I have T-shirts, _____ , and my sandals . . . I'm so excited!

Juliet: But, Kyle, San Francisco is cold and _____ in the summer.

Kyle: Really? But San Francisco is in California! It's always sunny there!

Juliet: No, it's not. _____ is _____ and sunny, but not _____ .

Kyle: Oh . . .

Juliet: You should take some sweaters and long _____ , too.

Kyle: Oh, OK. Good idea.

B   Practice the conversation with a partner.

5 Speaking Strategy

Role play. Choose a situation below and create a short role play. Do steps 1 and 2. Then switch roles.

1. Student A: Give advice to your partner in two different ways.

2. Student B: Refuse the advice the first time. Then accept it.

Useful Expressions

Giving advice

	Accepting	Refusing
(I think) you should take a sweater.	Good idea. OK, I will.	Really? I don't think so. Really? I'd rather not.
I don't think you should drive. You shouldn't drive.	You're probably right.	Really? I think I'll be OK.

1. Your partner is going to a party. It's snowing hard and the roads aren't safe. Your partner wants to drive to the party anyway.

2. Your partner wants to have a picnic on Saturday. The weather forecast is for rain all day.

3. You and your partner are at the beach. It's very hot and sunny. Your partner sunburns easily and he/she wants to go swimming immediately.

4. Your partner wants to go jogging on a chilly day. He's / She's wearing shorts and a T-shirt.

Example: A: It's snowing outside. I don't think you should drive.
           B: Really? I think I'll be OK. I'm a good driver.
           A: But the roads aren't safe. You should probably take the subway.
           B: Hmm. . . OK, I will. Thanks.

6 Language Link   Connecting sentences with *but, or, so*

A   Study the chart. Then complete the sentences below with *but, or,* or *so.*

It's cold **but** sunny in Vancouver today. It's cold in Boston, **but** it's warm in Miami.	• shows an opposite or contrast • joins words and sentences
Is it warm **or** chilly today? It's very hot! I can't eat **or** sleep. We can go to the beach, **or** we can visit the zoo.	• gives a choice • joins words, phrases, and sentences
It's raining, **so** we're not having a picnic in the park.	• gives a result • joins sentences

1. William can't speak French, _____ Marion can.

2. Roberto is very healthy. He doesn't drink _____ smoke.

3. I feel tired, _____ I'm going home.

4. Does the movie start at 7:00 _____ 7:30?

5. Tokyo is an exciting city, _____ it's very expensive to live in.

6. The computer is broken, _____ I can't check my e-mail.

7. It's cold outside, _____ Mario is wearing shorts.

8. For dinner, you can have chicken, fish, _____ beef.

B   Combine the two sentences using *but, or,* or *so.*

1. Damon likes to travel. His girlfriend doesn't like to travel.

   Damon likes to travel, but his girlfriend doesn't. _____

2. We can go to Martin's party. We can see a movie.

   _____

3. John is sick. He's not coming to class today.

   _____

4. It's a beautiful day. We're having class outside.

   _____

5. I'm wearing my glasses. I can't see the whiteboard.

   _____

6. Alain wants to study at an American university. He's taking the TOEFL exam.

   _____

C   Complete the sentences about yourself. Then read each sentence to a partner.
Your partner asks you one question about each sentence.

1. I can _____ , but I can't _____ .

2. I like to _____ or _____ in the summer.

3. The weather here is often _____ in the summer, so _____

7 Communication Where should I go?

 A Interview your partner. Complete the survey with his or her answers.

Vacation Survey

1. I usually take a vacation in the _____ .
   ❏ spring   ❏ autumn
   ❏ summer   ❏ winter

2. I like _____ weather.
   ❏ hot
   ❏ warm
   ❏ cool
   ❏ other (your idea): _____

3. I like to _____ on vacation.
   ❏ relax
   ❏ exercise
   ❏ see things
   ❏ other: _____

4. What are your favorite activities?
   ❏ swimming   ❏ skiing   ❏ surfing

   ❏ hiking   ❏ golfing   ❏ mountain biking

   ❏ other: _____

 B Imagine that your partner is looking for a place to go on vacation.
Read about the places below and choose one for your partner.

Cape Town, South Africa

Weather:
- In spring and summer (September–March), it's warm.
- The autumn and winter months are chilly, and it rains.

Activities:
This coastal city has beautiful mountains and lovely beaches. They're great for
- hiking   • surfing
- swimming   • relaxing
- waterskiing

Las Vegas, USA

Weather:
- Sunny days, cool evenings all year.
- In summer, it's 100°F/38°C.

Activities:
- casinos, great nightlife and restaurants
- swimming pools and golf courses
- beautiful mountains for hiking, and for skiing and snowboarding in winter

Hokkaido, Japan

Weather:
- There's low humidity all year.
- Winters are cold.
- July and August are dry and beautiful.

Activities:
- Skiing is popular in winter.
- Summer is great for camping, hiking, and mountain biking.
- The popular Sapporo Snow Festival is held in February.

 C Tell your partner your suggestion. Explain your reasons. Does your partner like your suggestion?

> Let's see. . . . You usually take your vacation in the winter and you like hot weather, so you should . . .

 D Change partners, and do activities **A** to **C** again.

Vacation!

Lesson B On vacation

1 Vocabulary Link When you travel

A Imagine that you are going on vacation to another country. Match an activity with a photo.

a. ~~pack your suitcase~~   d. go sightseeing   g. show photos to friends
b. check into your hotel   e. get a passport   h. rent a car
c. buy a plane ticket   f. take photos   i. unpack

B Which activities do you do before you travel? Which do you do on vacation? Which ones do you do after the trip? Tell your partner.

ASK ANSWER

How often do you go on vacation? Do you have a passport? Why or why not? On vacation, do you take a lot of photos?

2 Listening   On vacation

A   Look at the five photos below. What do you think the people are doing?

B   Listen to three conversations. Match each conversation to a picture. Two of the pictures are extra.

CD 1
Track 25

C   Look at your answers (1, 2, 3) in **B**. What are the people doing?
Listen. You will hear three answers. Circle the correct answer.

CD 1
Track 26

1. A   B   C

2. A   B   C

3. A   B   C

D   Listen to the conversations in **B** again. Fill in the missing words to complete the requests.

CD 1
Track 25

1. _____ I _____ your passport, please?

2. _____ you take our _____ , please?

3. _____ I see a credit card and some form of _____ , please?

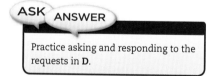

ASK ANSWER

Practice asking and responding to the requests in **D**.

3 Reading   A newspaper article

A   When you travel, do you ever forget things? What do you forget? Where do you forget them?
Compare your answers with a partner.

What	Where

B   Take 30 seconds and skim the article on p. 43. Choose the best title for it.

Old and New   Coming and Going   Lost and Found   In and Out

In Tokyo, it's an envelope with $850,000 in cash. At Florida's Disney World, it's a glass eye. At a hotel in England, it's a goat from a nearby farm.

How are all of these things similar? They are unusual things that people leave in hotel rooms, in airports, and on city streets.

Trish Martino works in the Lost and Found Center at an airport in a U.S. city. "Sure, we find the usual stuff—cell phones, keys, sunglasses, and wallets," she says. "But people also forget some weird things at the airport, too." What does Ms. Martino find? A woman's false teeth in the bathroom. A department store mannequin in an airport waiting area. "How do you forget those things?" Martino wonders. Nobuo Hasuda works for the Lost and Found Center in downtown Tokyo.

cash

a mannequin

a glass eye

false teeth

a goat

The Center has almost 800,000 items, and 300,000 of them are umbrellas! There are also many other things—jewelry and briefcases, snowshoes, and musical instruments.

Mr. Hasuda keeps the lost items for about 200 days. After this time, the finder can take the item. This is good luck for some people. Remember the envelope in Tokyo with $850,000? The owner did not claim it. Now the money belongs to the finder!

C Match the amounts on the left with what they describe on the right.

1. two hundred
2. eight hundred thousand
3. eight hundred fifty thousand
4. three hundred thousand

a. cash
b. days
c. lost items
d. umbrellas

D These sentences are false. Correct each one to make it true.

1. The article is about ~~typical~~ *unusual* things people leave behind.

2. Trish Martino works at a train station.

3. Trish says they find cell phones, keys, sunglasses, and purses.

4. The center in Tokyo has hundreds of thousands of briefcases.

5. After 200 days, the finder can buy the lost item.

ASK ANSWER

Did anything in the article surprise you? If so, what?

4 Language Link   *Whose; possessive pronouns; belong to*

A Study the chart. Notice the words in blue.

 Be careful! *Whose* asks about an owner.
Who's = Who is.

	Possessive adjectives	Possessive pronouns	*belong to*
Whose passport is this? PASSPORT	It's my passport. your her his our their	It's mine. yours. hers. his. ours. theirs.	It **belongs to** me. you. her. him. us. them.

B Use the chart in **A** to complete the conversation with the correct words. Then practice the conversation.

Jim: Well, I have (1) __my__ luggage. Where's (2) _____ ?

Ben: Um . . . let's see. . . . Oh, here's (3) _____ suitcase. No, wait . . . this one isn't (4) _____ .

Jim: (5) _____ is it?

Ben: It says Mr. Simon Konig. It belongs to (6) _____ .

Jim: Hey, I think that man has (7) _____ suitcase. See? He probably thinks it's (8) _____ .

Ben: I'll ask him. . . . Excuse me, does this suitcase belong to (9) _____ ?

Simon: Oh, sorry. My mistake! I thought it was (10) _____ !

C Read the sentences. Substitute a possessive pronoun for the underlined words. Then say the sentences aloud.

1. That's not her suitcase. <u>Her suitcase</u> is over there.   ____Hers____

2. Can I borrow your cell phone? <u>My cell phone</u> doesn't work.   _____

3. Is your class fun? <u>Their class</u> is interesting.   _____

4. Is your hometown hot in the summer? <u>Our hometown</u> really is!   _____

5. My birthday is in May. <u>Your birthday</u> is in March.   _____

D Read the directions to do this activity.

1. Student A closes his or her eyes.

2. Each of the other students chooses a personal item and puts it on Student A's desk.

3. Student A opens his or her eyes.

4. Student A guesses the owner of each item.

5. Repeat the activity with a different student playing the role of Student A.

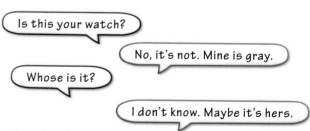

5 Writing   **Newspaper ad**

A   Read the ad below. Then write an ad about a lost item of yours.

> # LOST!
>
> Brown leather backpack. Two university textbooks are inside—
> one is a math textbook. The other is a history book. Lost at a bus
> stop near Georgetown University on Monday night. Please contact
> the owner at 555-2121. $50 reward!

B   Put your ad on the classroom wall. Read the other ads.
Are any of the ads similar? What kinds of things do most people lose?

6 Communication   **Are we compatible?**

A   Complete the survey below with your answers.

On vacation . . .	My answer	My partner's answer
1. How do you like to travel—by bus, plane, train, or car?		
2. How many suitcases do you usually take?		
3. What is something you always take? What is something you never take?		
4. Do you spend a lot of money?		
5. Do you like to travel by yourself or go with a group?		
6. Do you like to take a lot of pictures?		
7. Do you like to go sightseeing or relax?		

B   Get together with a partner. Take turns asking and answering the questions. Explain your answers.

C   Are you and your partner similar or different?
Do you think you could travel together?
Why or why not? Tell the class.

> My partner likes to travel by bus,
> but I don't. I like to travel by car.

Check out the World Link video.

Practice your English online at http://elt.heinle.com/worldlink

5 Heroes

Lesson A Risk-takers

1 Vocabulary Link   Two people changing their world

A   Look at the blue words in **B**. How many do you know?

B   Read these two profiles. Answer the questions with a partner.

	present		past
	is	→	was
	are	→	were

1. When or where was the person born?
2. What is the person's job?
3. What does the person want to do?

(handwritten: Iran ambassador writer / space ambassador writer / write the best speeches)

Anousheh Ansari   *space ambassador*

Jon Favreau   *writer*

Anousheh Ansari was born in Iran. As a teenager, she moved to the United States. She is the co-founder, with a friend, of an internet company. She is also a popular speaker around the world.

More importantly, in 2006 Ansari realized her childhood dream: She was the first female private space explorer. It was so exciting to be a space traveler!

Now she wants to help bring peace to the world as the world's first "space ambassador[1]"—a kind of teacher about outer space.

Her motto: "Be the change you want to see in the world." (Gandhi)

[1]ambassador = a person who represents a country or a cause

In college, Jon Favreau was the editor[2] of his school's newspaper. He studied classical piano. He didn't become a musician, though. He is a speechwriter.

Every politician needs a good writer. Jon Favreau is the Director (top manager) of Speechwriting for Barack Obama, President of the United States.

For Obama's speeches, Favreau works as a researcher first. He reads and studies a lot before he writes. He wants to write the best speeches possible.

He was born in 1981, and has a long career ahead of himself!

[2]editor = the top person at a newspaper or magazine

C   Write the blue words in **B** in the correct column. Can you add any words?

-ER	-OR	-IST	-IAN
lawyer	doctor	activist	physician
traveler teacher			

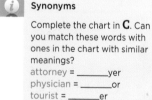

Synonyms

Complete the chart in **C**. Can you match these words with ones in the chart with similar meanings?
attorney = _____yer
physician = _____or
tourist = _____er
instructor = _____er

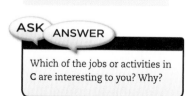

ASK ANSWER

Which of the jobs or activities in **C** are interesting to you? Why?

2 Listening   **A dangerous job**

> Look at the places on the map below. What do you know about these places?

CD 1
Track 27

A A radio announcer is interviewing Alejandro about his job.
Listen to the interview and answer the question.

Where in the world is Alejandro? Circle it on the map.

B Listen again. What job(s) does Alejandro do? Circle your answer(s).

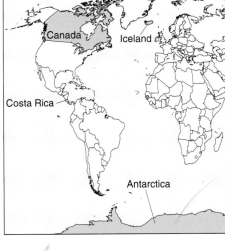

Canada   Iceland

Costa Rica

Antarctica

photographer

journalist

ski instructor

explorer

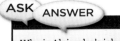

ASK ANSWER

Why is Alejandro's job
dangerous? Is his job
interesting to you? Can you
name other dangerous jobs?

CD 1
Track 27

C Listen again. What does Alejandro say? Complete the sentences by circling the correct words.

1. Sometimes my camera breaks / freezes.

2. Today it's -13 / -30.

3. I was born in Costa Rica / Canada.

4. It's a quiet / nice place.

5. I write for a newspaper / online.

3 Pronunciation   **Showing surprise**

CD 1
Track 28

A Listen to these sentences. Notice the sentence stress and intonation. Then practice saying them.

1. A: Sometimes my camera freezes.

   B: <u>Really</u>? How cold does it get?

2. A: Today it's minus 30 degrees.

   B: <u>You're kidding</u>! Now *that's* cold!

B Tell your group something surprising about yourself. Other members
of the group will respond with an expression in the box.

> Really?   Yeah?   You're kidding!   No way!

A: I have a twin brother.

B: Really? I didn't know that.

C: You're kidding! What's his name?

4 Speaking **You must really like it.**

CD 1
Track 29

A Listen to the conversation. Then follow these two steps and answer the questions.

1. Find a word that means *not afraid*.

2. Find a word that means *a movie that shows real events*.

3. Do Kurt and Maggie like the movie? How do you know?

Kurt: Hey, Maggie. What movie are you watching tonight?

Maggie: It's a documentary. It's called *Man on Wire*. It's my second time watching it.

Kurt: *Man on Wire*. . . . Hmm. . . .

Maggie: Do you know it?

Kurt: Yeah, I do. It's a great movie.

Maggie: I agree. The guy in the movie was really brave.

Kurt: Oh, I know. And it was in New York. I love New York City!

Maggie: Me, too. Hey, do you want to watch the movie with me?

Kurt: Again? Well . . . . sure. Why not?

B Practice the conversation with a partner.

5 Speaking Strategy

A Complete the chart with information about two movies you like.

name of movie	actor(s) in movie	words that describe movie
hang over 2		
Michon impasoplez	Tom Cruz	It's an action movie talking about

B Tell your partner about your movie. Use the language in the box to help you.

A: I think *Pink Panther 2* is a good movie.

B: Yeah, I agree. It's really fun.

C: Really? I don't think so.

A: Why do you say that?

C: It's too long and it's not that funny.

Useful Expressions		
Agreeing or disagreeing with an opinion		
Statement: I think *Man on Wire* is a good movie.		**Follow-up questions**
Agreeing	Yeah, I agree. I know. Yeah, you're right.	What do you like about it?
Disagreeing	Really? I don't think so. Sorry, but I disagree. I don't really agree.	Why do you say that?

6 Language Link   The past tense of *be*: statements and *yes / no* questions

A   Use the words in the box to complete the chart. Pay attention to the verb forms in the chart.

	subject		be		
ago in She They was weren't	I / He / _She_ / It		_was_ wasn't	there _in_ 2007. on TV last night.	
	You / We / _They_		were _weren't_	famous two years _ago_ .	

B   Complete the conversation with a partner. Use the correct form of the verb *be* in the past tense.

Tim: Hi, Kelly. It's Tim. I called you yesterday, but you (not) (1) _wasn't_ home.

Kelly: I (2) _was_ at the library. I'm writing a paper about Pierre and Marie Curie.

Tim: They (3) _are_ scientists from France, right?

Kelly: Right. Well, actually Pierre (4) _his_ French, but his wife (not) (5) _didn't_ born in France. She (6) _wasn't_ from Poland. She (7) _were_ also the first person to win a Nobel Prize twice.

Pioneers in Science

C   Complete the chart with your birth year (1). For 2–5 write information about yourself three years ago. Then tell a partner about yourself.

1. birth year	2. job	3. feeling/situation	4. place	5. relationship
1994	student	busy	Taipei	single

I was born in 1994. Three years ago I was a student. I was busy. I was in Taipei. Of course I was single!

Yes / No Questions	Answers
Were you born in Mexico?	Yes, I was. / No, I wasn't. I was born in Spain.
Was Ms. Jones your teacher?	Yes, she was. / No, she wasn't. Mr. Davis was.

D   Ask another partner yes/no questions about the personal information in **C**. Take turns.

Three years ago, were you happy?

No, I wasn't. I was busy studying for exams!

7 Communication   Who are we going to invite?

A Read the headings in the chart. Then think of famous people you know and complete the chart. The people can be from the past or present. Share your answers with a partner.

Entertainers*	BoB marly
Leaders	
Thinkers	inishtine
Explorers	Colompos
Activists	geivara
(Other: your idea)	

* = singers, actors, musicians, etc.

Junko Tabai, first woman to climb Mount Everest

B Use your information in **A** and follow these steps.

1. You are going to have a dinner party. You can invite four famous people from the past or present.

2. Complete the chart with the names and occupations of the people you want to invite.

3. List your reasons for inviting them.

1.	Person:	BoB marly.
	Job:	singer
	Reason:	I like him. because his my best singer.
2.	Person:	obama.
	Job:	
	Reason:	
3.	Person:	king abdullah
	Job:	
	Reason:	
4.	Person:	Tom cruz.
	Job:	
	Reason:	

C Get into a group of three people. Compare your answers in **B**. Explain your choices. Together, make one list of four people to invite to the party.

> I think we should invite Bob Marley. He was a great musician and a peace activist.

> Yeah, I agree. Let's invite him.

Heroes

Lesson B Personal heroes

1 Vocabulary Link   Who is your personal hero?

> Find the word *hero* in your dictionary. Then answer this question:
> What kinds of things does a hero do? Make a list.

Notice!

He works <u>for</u> himself. = He
      doesn't work for a company.
I live <u>by</u> myself. = I live alone.

A Read the question and Alice's and Jenny's answers. Then circle the correct words to complete
the definitions.

> Who is your personal hero?

> I admire Grace Gobbo. I think she's a great
> woman. She works as a scientist in Tanzania. There
> are more than 10,000 kinds of plants in Tanzania.
> Grace works with traditional doctors and studies
> the plants they use. She takes the doctors' ideas
> and puts them into a computer database. Just
> like Grace, I want to work for the Jane Goodall
> Institute. I'm looking forward to meeting Grace
> one day!

Jenny

Jimmy Chin

> I look up to Jimmy Chin. He's a mountain
> climber and he works as a photojournalist. He
> works for himself—he's very independent. He
> travels around the world and takes photos.
> He's always looking for the best picture. He
> has photos online from Mali, Mexico, Pakistan,
> and China. I think Jimmy's good at his job, and
> also brave!

Alice

Grace Gobbo

1. If you *look forward to* something, you are worried / excited about it happening in the future.

2. If you *look up to* someone, you admire / dislike the person.

3. If you *look for* something, you try to find / lose the thing.

B Describe your dream job. What kind of work do you do? Complete the chart.
Then share your answers with a partner.

work as	_____
	(job)
work for	_____
	(company)
work with	_____
	(people, things)

> My dream is to work with
> animals. I want to work as a . . .

C Complete the sentences with information about your personal hero:

I look up to _____ . I admire this person because _____ .

2 Listening The night shift

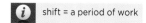 *shift = a period of work*

A Look at the work shifts below.
Can you name a job for each shift?
What are the good and bad things
about each shift?

1st shift: 8 a.m.–4 p.m.

2nd shift: 4 p.m.–12 a.m.

3rd (night) shift: 12 a.m.–8 a.m.

> **Complete this list:**
> 1st = first
> 2nd = second
> 3rd = _____
> 4th = _____
> 5th = _____

CD 1
Track 30

B Listen to this conversation at a party.
What is Lindsay's schedule? Circle your answer.
(W = work day; F = free day)

1. W   W   F   F   W   W   F   F
2. W   W   W   W   F   F   F   F
3. W   F   F   W   W   F   F   W

CD 1
Track 30

C Listen again. Complete the sentences by matching.
Answers may be used more than once. Two
answers are extra.

1. Lindsay works at a ____b____ .   a. clinic
2. She works as a ____d____ .   b. hospital
3. She starts work at ____e____ .   c. doctor
4. She finishes work at ____g____ .   d. nurse
5. Ben works as a ____c____ .   e. 8 a.m.
6. He works at a ____b____ .   f. 4 p.m.
7. He finishes work at ____e____ .   g. 8 p.m.

Some taxi drivers work the night shift.

D What are the good things about Lindsay's and Ben's jobs? What are the bad things?
Make a list and then compare ideas with a partner.

3 Reading Making a difference

A Scan the reading quickly and find the six places (cities, areas, and countries) mentioned.

Where are these places? Can you find them on a map? What do you know about these places?

B Scan the reading on page 53. Complete these sentences about Hector Sierra below.

1. Hector Sierra works as an ____activist____ and an _____ .
2. He works for an organization called _____ .
3. He works with _____ . He wants them to learn about another _____ .
4. He believes in world _____ .

Making a difference

Hector Sierra, a native of Colombia, is talking with a group of news reporters about his organization, Artists Without Borders. One reporter asks, "What exactly is AWB?" Sierra thinks for a moment, and then says, "I guess Artists Without Borders is a Colombian guy teaching Japanese culture to kids around the world . . ."

The story of Artists Without Borders begins in Tokyo, where Sierra was a graduate student of film at Nihon University. As a student, Sierra visited Kosovo. He wanted to make a movie about the war there. The war made Sierra very sad. He wanted to help the people—especially the children of the area.

Sierra returned to Japan and started Artists Without Borders. He wanted to bring some happiness to the children of Kosovo, using art. Three months later, Sierra was back in Kosovo with crayons, origami paper, and paints. He started working with the children.

Since then, Artists Without Borders has visited other troubled places, including Chechnya and Afghanistan. In each place, Sierra works with children on two main projects—drawing and origami. Through drawing, the kids can show their hopes and fears. By working with origami paper, the children learn to make their own toys.

Sierra wants all of the projects to be fun. But he also hopes the children learn about another culture. This, he believes, is a first step toward world peace.

C What happened in these places in Hector's life? Complete the chart.

Colombia	He was born there.
Tokyo	He studied
Kosovo	
Afghanistan	

D Think of a good project for Artists Without Borders. Complete the sentence below. Give details to your partner.

My project idea: Artists Without Borders should visit _____ because _____ .

What year did the volunteer organization *Doctors Without Borders* begin offering free medical help worldwide?
a. 1971
b. 1987
c. 1994

4 Language Link   The simple past: regular verbs and *wh-* questions with *be*

A   Say the words and sentences in the chart. Pay attention to the verb forms.

Simple past: Regular verbs		
I / You / He / She / We / They	visited didn't visit	Mexico last month.

move → move**d**
visit → visit**ed**
play → play**ed**
study → stud**ied**
stop → stop**ped**

B   Complete Alec's story with the simple past tense form of the verbs. Pay attention to spelling.

Help from a Stranger

There was a girl named Alyssa in my class. I (1. like) _liked_ her a lot. I was shy, but one day I (2. invite) _invited_ her to have dinner with me the next weekend at a nice restaurant.

After dessert, I (3. ask) _asked_ our friendly waiter for the check. I (4. offer) _offered_ to pay. I (5. look) _looked_ in my wallet. I had only ten dollars. I (6. not have) _didn't have_ enough money!

I went to the men's room. I (7. try) _tried_ to call my roommate. I (8. wait) _waited_ , but he (9. not answer) _didn't answer_ the phone. I left a message, and (10. explain) _explained_ the situation.

Just then, the bathroom door (11. open) _opened_. It was my waiter. He (12. hand) _handed_ me $20. I (13. promise) _promised_ to pay him back. He (14. reply) _replied_ , "Don't worry about it."

C   Look at the chart below. Notice the two question forms.

Yes / No question		Was	Alec	shy?	Yes, he was. / No, he wasn't.
Wh- question	Why	was	Alec	shy?	(He was shy) because he liked Alyssa.

D   Complete the *wh-* questions with the question words in the box. Take turns asking and answering the questions.

> who   what   when   where   why

1. _When_ was the dinner date?
2. _____ was Alyssa?
3. _____ was friendly?
4. _____ was Alec worried?

5. _____ was in Alec's wallet?
6. _____ was Alec after dinner?
7. _____ was in the waiter's hand?
8. At the end, _____ was Alec happy?

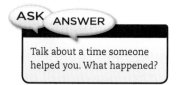

ASK ANSWER

Talk about a time someone helped you. What happened?

5 Writing **My hero**

A Complete the writing sample with the correct past tense forms of the verbs.

B Write your own paragraph about your hero.

 C Share your writing with a partner. Ask your partner about his or her hero.

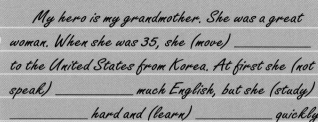

My hero is my grandmother. She was a great woman. When she was 35, she (move) _____ to the United States from Korea. At first she (not speak) _____ much English, but she (study) _____ hard and (learn) _____ quickly. When she was 46, she (start) _____ her own business. She (work) _____ for herself. She was very smart!

My grandmother (die) _____ five years ago, but I still admire her. She was a very brave and strong woman. She is my personal hero.

6 Communication **Hero of the Year**

A Every year, your city gives a Hero of the Year award to one person. This year, there are three choices. Read about each person. Who is your choice? Why?

Carson McClure, 30

Carson McClure works for himself. He has a successful design company and he makes a lot of money. This year he is giving ten poor children $10,000 each for college.

Amanda Conrey, 54

On the night of June 24, Amanda Conrey heard a loud explosion. In front of her house, a car was on fire. A child was in the car. Amanda pulled the child out of the car. She saved the little boy's life.

Logan Myers, 22

When he was 16, Logan was in a car accident. Now he is in a wheelchair. This year, he climbed 3,776 meters to the top of Mount Fuji using special ropes. "It was very difficult," says Myers, "but I did it." And now Logan is looking forward to his next challenge: Mount Everest.

 B Get into a group of three or four people. Who is your choice? Why do you admire this person? Explain your answer to the group.

 C As a group, choose one person to get the award. Explain your answer to the class.

 Check out the World Link video.   Practice your English online at http://elt.heinle.com/worldlink

1 Vocabulary Link Can you remember?

> **OPPOSITES**
>
> remember ←——→ forget
> (to keep information   (to not
> in your mind)   remember)

A How good is your memory? Take this quiz.

	Yes	No
1. I sometimes forget to do my homework.	☐	☐
2. I never forget my cell phone.	☐	☐
3. I forget names easily.	☐	☐
4. I need to write important things down or I forget them.	☐	☐
5. I'm good at remembering the words to songs.	☐	☐
6. I can remember most of the details when I look at a picture only once.	☐	☐
7. It's important to remember your parents' birthdays, but sometimes I forget.	☐	☐

B Circle your answer. Give a reason for your answer based on **A**.

I have a good / bad memory.

A: I think I have a good memory.

B: Really? Why?

A: Well, I don't forget names easily. And I'm good at remembering the words to songs. I love music!

C Use one of the examples below or your own idea. Make notes in the chart about a day in your life you will never forget.

> **I'll never forget the day. . . .**
> I met my boyfriend/girlfriend.   I took the university entrance exam.
> I graduated from school.   your idea: _____

When was it?	
Where were you?	
What happened?	
Why was it special?	

 D Share your answers from **C**.

> I'll *never forget* the day I took the university entrance exam. It was two years ago. I was nervous and I couldn't remember the answers . . .

2 Listening   There are things you can do.

A How do you remember new words in English? Tell one idea to a partner.

CD 1
Track 31

B Listen to part of Galina and Tomo's conversation. Circle the correct answer to complete the sentence.

They're talking about an English _____ .

a. word   b. test   c. teacher

CD 1
Track 32

C Listen to the entire conversation. Look at the pictures. Check (✓) the things Galina does. Then circle the correct answer to the question.

Why is Tomo worried?

a. He thinks he did poorly.

b. He just got a bad grade.

c. He has a lot of homework.

ASK ANSWER

Which method in C do you think is best? Why?

3 Pronunciation   The past tense -ed ending

CD 1
Track 33

A Listen to and say the words in the chart. Pay attention to the pronunciation of the -ed ending.

/t/	/d/	/ɪd/
watched	studied	wanted
liked	explained	decided

CD 1
Track 34

B What is the final sound of each verb? Circle your answers.

1. We walked home.   /t/ /ɪd/
2. They moved to Taipei.   /d/ /ɪd/
3. It started to rain.   /d/ /ɪd/
4. You finished on time.   /t/ /ɪd/
5. I added a word to the list. /d/ /ɪd/
6. We laughed loudly.   /t/ /ɪd/

7. We enjoyed the visit.   /d/ /ɪd/
8. He needed help.   /t/ /ɪd/
9. They learned the song.   /d/ /ɪd/
10. Mom asked a question.   /t/ /ɪd/
11. She remembered me.   /d/ /ɪd/
12. I hated math class.   /t/ /ɪd/

4 Speaking   Maybe. I'm not sure.

A Listen to Mia and Justin's conversation. Where do you think they're going? What is Justin looking for?

CD 1
Track 35

Mia: I'm so excited! Are you ready to go in?

Justin: Um, . . . just a minute. I can't find the tickets.

Mia: You're kidding!

Justin: No, I'm not. I put them in my front pocket. See? They're not there.

Mia: Well, are they in your backpack?

Justin: I don't think so.

Mia: Maybe you dropped them somewhere.

Justin: Maybe. I'm not sure.

Mia: Oh, Justin. What are we going to do?

Justin: Wait . . . hold on. I found them. They were in my *back* pocket.

Mia: Great! Let's go!

B Practice the conversation with a partner.

5 Speaking Strategy

Take turns asking and answering the questions with a partner. Use the Useful Expressions in your answers.

your teacher	your partner
Is your teacher married? Does your teacher like vegetables? your question: _____	Does your partner live near you? Does your partner like rap music? your question: _____
your school	**public schools in the U.S.**
Are there a lot of restaurants near your school? Is there a bus stop near your school? your question: _____	Do students wear uniforms? Does the school year start in the fall? your question: _____

Useful Expressions

Expressing degrees of certainty

Are they in your backpack?
  Yes, they are. / No, they aren't.
  (very certain)

  I think so. / I don't think so.
  (less certain)

  Maybe. I'm not sure.
  (not very certain)

  I have no idea.
  (= I don't know.)

6 Language Link   The simple past: irregular verbs

A Study the sentences in the chart. Pay attention to the verb forms.

Simple past: Irregular verbs	
I Carlos My parents	forgot the tickets at home. didn't forget the tickets at home.

B What are the past forms of these verbs? Work together with a partner to write the answers. Check your answers on page 149.

1. break   _broke_
2. begin   _____
3. come   _____
4. do   _____
5. fall   _____
6. feel   _____
7. go   _____

8. have   _____
9. know   _____
10. make   _____
11. run   _____
12. say   _____
13. shake   _____
14. think   _____

C Complete the story below with the past form of the verbs in parentheses. Some verbs are regular and some are irregular.

An Unforgettable Night

When I (1. be) _____ in high school,
there (2. be) _____ a terrible earthquake.
I will always remember that day. It (3. begin)
_____ early in the morning. At 2:00
a.m., I (4. be) _____ in bed. Suddenly, I
(5. feel) _____ my bed move. Just then,
my brother (6. come) _____ into my room
and (7. yell) _____ , "It's an earthquake!"
The room (8. shake) _____ very hard. I
(9. not know) _____ what to do. I (10. run)
_____ under a table. Books (11. fall) _____ from the shelves. Glasses (12. break)
_____ on the floor. After about half a minute, the shaking (13. stop) _____ . My brother
and I (14. not say) _____ anything. We (15. go) _____ into the kitchen. There (16. be)
_____ glass everywhere. I (17. turn on) _____ the radio. The announcer (18. say)
_____ , "A 7.6 earthquake hit the city!"

D Take turns reading the story in **C** with a partner. Then explain the story in your own words.

7 Communication   Early memories

A   What are some of your childhood memories? Make notes about your ideas in the chart.

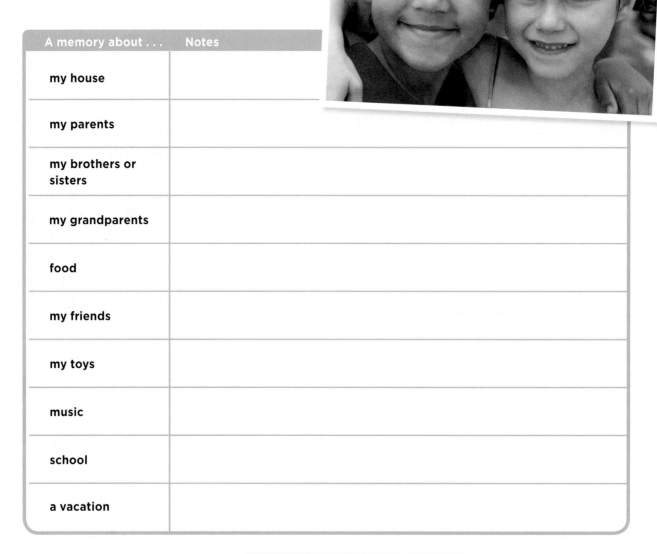

A memory about . . .	Notes
my house	
my parents	
my brothers or sisters	
my grandparents	
food	
my friends	
my toys	
music	
school	
a vacation	

> As a child, I lived with my family in a small apartment. The apartment building had a big yard. I played there with my sister . . .

 B   Get together with a partner. Take turns telling each other your memories.

 C   Discuss the questions with your partner.

    1. Are any of your memories similar to your partner's?

    2. Which memory is your favorite?

 D   Share your partner's favorite memory with the class.

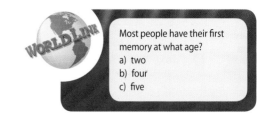

WORLD LINK

Most people have their first memory at what age?
a) two
b) four
c) five

The Mind

1 Vocabulary Link **Sleepwalking**

A Look at the picture. What do you think is happening? Tell a partner.

B Read this story about two brothers, Harry and Oskar. Use the words in the box to complete the story. Answer the questions.

day   night   asleep

1. When did Harry and Oskar go to bed?

2. What did Oskar do?

This is a funny story that happened the (1) _____day_____ before yesterday (two days ago).

It was Thursday evening. My brother, Oskar, went to bed at 10:30.

I go to school during the (2) _____ and then study at (3) _____ , so I stayed up late. I went to bed at midnight, and I fell (4) _____ at about 1:00.

In the middle of the (5) _____ (at 3:30 a.m.), I heard a noise and I woke up. I could hear the sound of typing. I got up and walked into the other room.

I saw Oskar sitting at the computer! He was emailing his friends. "What are you doing?" I asked. Oskar didn't say anything. Oskar was still (6) _____ . He was sleepwalking! I didn't want to wake him up. "Go back to sleep, Oskar," I said. And he did.

The next (7) _____ , Oskar didn't remember anything!

C Look at the expressions in blue in **B**. Complete the chart with opposites.

go to bed	get up
wake up	
	at night
at noon	
	the day after tomorrow

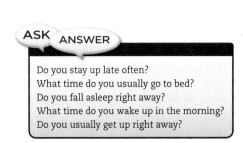

ASK ANSWER

Do you stay up late often?
What time do you usually go to bed?
Do you fall asleep right away?
What time do you wake up in the morning?
Do you usually get up right away?

2 Listening **A nighttime story**

Do you know any stories about sleepwalkers? What happened?

CD 1
Track 36

A Circle the correct answer.

You are listening to _____ .

a. a TV show   c. a conversation between friends

b. a lecture   d. radio news

B What did Mary do? Place a check mark (✓) in the correct box.

CD 1
Track 37

C Listen again. Put the events in order.

__1__ Mary went to bed at 10:00.   _____ Mary tried to buy ice cream.

_____ The police drove Mary home.   _____ Mary drove away.

_____ She got up in the middle of the night.   _____ The police woke Mary up.

D Tell a partner Mary's story. Use your own words.

3 Reading **Sleep patterns**

A Discuss the questions with a partner. Then compare your answers with the class.

1. How many hours do you sleep each night?

2. What do you do when you can't sleep?

B Read the article. What is the main point of the article? Circle the best sentence.

1. Today people have healthier sleep patterns.
2. Waking up at night can make you sick.
3. It's normal not to sleep through the night.
4. Sleep research has a lot of problems.

A STUDY OF SLEEP

It's 3:30 in the morning. Tomorrow is a busy day. You went to bed at 10:00. You need to get up at 6:00 in the morning. But you woke up in the middle of the night and you can't fall back asleep! You're frustrated. Why can't you sleep properly?

There may be a surprising answer. Dr. Thomas Wehr did some research on sleep. During the winter, he put people in a room with no artificial light (there was no light from lamps, TVs, or computers). Then he studied the people's sleep patterns.

What happened? The people went to bed, but they didn't fall asleep right away. Most were awake for two hours. Next, the people slept for four to five hours. Then they woke up and they stayed awake and were active for one to three hours. Finally, the people slept again for four to five hours.

Dr. Wehr discovered a new sleep pattern. But maybe it's not new. In the past, before electric light, perhaps people slept this way. Nowadays, we sleep in a different way.

So, the next time you wake up in the middle of the night and can't sleep, relax! Your sleep patterns may be normal after all!

C Read about Thomas Wehr's research. Then complete the table below about sleep patterns.

SLEEP PATTERNS	
People are in bed but are awake.	2 hours
People sleep.	
	1–3 hours
	4–5 hours

> **ASK ANSWER**
> What do you think of the sleep pattern described in this article? Is it healthy? Why or why not?

4 Language Link   The simple past: question forms

A Study the chart. Then complete the conversation below with the correct past tense questions and answers. Use the words in parentheses.

	Yes/No questions	Answers	Wh- questions	Answers
Regular verbs	Did you study for the test?	Yes, I did. No, I didn't.	When did you study?	Last night.
Irregular verbs	Did you forget the tickets?		Where did you forget the tickets?	At home.

Jay: Hey, Mario. (1. you/go) _____ *Did you go* _____ to the movies last night?

Mario: No, (2.) _____ . I rented a movie, instead.

Jay: Oh? What (3. you/rent) _____ ?

Mario: The movie *28 Days Later*.

Jay: (4. you/like) _____ it?

Mario: Yes, (5.) _____ , but after watching it, I (6. have) _____ nightmares.

Jay: Why (7. you/have) _____ nightmares?

Mario: Because it was a really scary movie. So, what (8. you/do) _____ last night?

Jay: I (9. go) _____ to a party with some friends.

Mario: Who (10. you/go) _____ with?

Jay: Margo and Antonia.

Mario: (11. you/have) _____ fun?

Jay: Yeah. We (12. have) _____ a great time.

B Practice the conversation in **A** with a partner.

C Unscramble these sentences. Then take turns asking your partner the questions.

1. what / get / you / up / did / time   _____

2. breakfast / did / this / have / morning / you   _____

3. time / arrive / here / you / did / what   _____

4. study / did / you / yesterday   _____

5. last / go / did / when / you / bed / to / night   _____

6. last / sleep / many / night / hours / you / how / did   _____

7. anywhere / did / go / you / your / vacation / on / summer   _____

> **What time did you get up?**

> **I overslept. I didn't get up until 7:45.**

5 Writing   **Staying up late**

A   Write about the last time you stayed up late. What did you do?

B   Exchange papers with a partner. Ask your partner a question about his or her writing.

> What's your favorite video game?

Last Saturday I stayed up late. I watched TV until 10:00 and then I played video games until about 12:30. I went to bed at 1:00. I couldn't fall asleep! The next morning, I slept in. I didn't get up until 11:00. I felt great, but my Dad wasn't happy. He says I'm lazy!

6 Communication   **Draw and guess!**

A   Complete these questions with the missing words.

1. How _____ you celebrate your birthday last year?

2. _____ did you grow up?

3. Where did you _____ on your last trip?

4. What _____ you do the day before _____ ?

5. Who _____ you _____ breakfast with this morning?

B   Play a guessing game. Read the rules below.

1. Ask your partner the first question in **A**.

2. Your partner draws his or her answer quickly.

3. Your partner cannot speak. Your partner cannot use numbers or letters when drawing.

4. Look at your partner's drawing. Guess the answer as fast as possible.

5. After you guess the first answer, move on to the next question.

6. The first team to finish all six questions wins the game!

C   Play the guessing game again. Switch roles with your partner.

> How did you celebrate your birthday last year? OK . . . Let's see. . . . Umm . . . I know! You had birthday cake with your family!

 Check out the World Link video.   Practice your English online at http://elt.heinle.com/worldlink

Review: Units 4–6

1 Storyboard

 A Vivian and Jun are visiting a museum. Look at the pictures and work with a partner to complete the conversations. More than one answer may be possible for each blank.

 B Practice the conversation with a partner. Then switch roles and practice again.

2 See It and Say It

A   Study the picture below for 15 seconds. Then, close your book.
What are the people doing? Tell your partner.

B   Talk about the picture.

- Where are these people?

- What season is it? How's the weather?

- Do you know any vacation resorts like this one? Where are they? What are they like?

C   Choose one pair of people in the picture. With a partner,
role play a conversation between the two people.

3 Memory Game

A Play a memory game. Read the instructions below.

Player A: Study the words and numbers in the chart below for 15 seconds.
Then close your book and draw the chart on a separate piece of paper.

Player B: Check Player A's answers.

breezy	68
fall asleep	go sightseeing
job	day
529	work for
passport	musician

B Play the game again. Switch roles. Use the chart below.

artist	cool
explorer	memory
313	myself
should	sleep late
47	unpack

C Answer the questions with a partner.

Could you remember most of the words when you looked at the chart only once?
Which words were easy to remember? Why? Which ones did you forget?

D Choose four words from each chart and use them in sentences.

4 Listen and Circle

CD 1
Track 38

You will hear a question and then four responses about each photo.
Circle the letter that best answers the question.

1.

A   B   C   D

2.

A   B   C   D

3.

A   B   C   D

5 Speak for a Minute!

A   Read the questions and think about your answers.

1. What's your favorite season? Why? What's the weather like?

2. How did you prepare for your last trip?

3. Describe three things that belong to you.

4. Describe your early years (ages 0–5).   **I was born in . . .**

5. What are two interesting jobs?

6. Who do you admire?

7. Talk about when you forgot something. What happened?

8. Talk about a time when you slept late. What happened?

B   Get into a group of three people.

1. Take turns. Choose a question, 1 to 8.

2. Answer the question by talking for one minute without stopping, and you get one point.

3. Continue until there are no more questions.

4. The winner is the person with the most points.

1 Vocabulary Link Adam's day

A Look at the pictures and read about Adam's day. Circle the places he visits in his neighborhood.

 neighborhood = **the area around your home**

Before school

This morning I was running late. I **skipped** breakfast, bought a cup of coffee and a newspaper, and got on the train for school.

After school, I **worked out** at the gym and bought a book. My friends went to the movies, but I didn't go with them. I went home to study!

After school

B Read about Adam's day again. Look at the words and pictures in **A**. Find words that have the same meaning.

 Word Partnerships

coffee shop / **copy** shop
bookstore / **grocery** store
train station / **police** station
hair salon / **nail** salon
newsstand / **taxi** stand
health club / **night**club

Find another word for . . .

1. exercised ___worked out___

2. coffee shop _____

3. cash machine _____

4. health club _____

5. missed _____

6. kiosk _____

ASK ANSWER

Which places do you go to? How often do you go there?
Which ones do your parents go to?

2 Listening Is this your neighborhood?

A Match the activities with all the places where you can do them. What other things can you do at these places?

> drink coffee   read   sleep
> play video games   shop   talk on your cell phone

Internet cafe

subway

library

bookstore

CD 2
Track 2

B Read the sentences below and then listen to Yuki and Pablo's conversation. Look at the underlined words. Change only the ones that are wrong.

1. Pablo is going to the <u>library</u> to <u>get a book</u>.

2. Yuki is going to the <u>bookstore</u> to buy a <u>DVD</u>.

3. Yuki and Pablo go to the <u>cafe</u> to <u>drink coffee and study</u>.

ASK ANSWER

Where do you usually drink coffee? study? buy books or magazines?

CD 2
Track 2

C Look at the chart. Can you guess the answers? Listen again and complete the chart with other ways of saying these ideas.

Original idea	What you hear
How are you?	~~how's it~~ going?
Is this your neighborhood?	~~Do~~ you ~~live~~ around here?
Where are you going?	Where are you ~~off to~~?
drink coffee	~~have~~ a cup of coffee

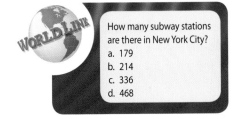

WORLD LINK

How many subway stations are there in New York City?
a. 179
b. 214
c. 336
d. 468

3 Pronunciation Stress in three-syllable words

CD 2
Track 3

A Listen to these sentences. Notice the stress of the underlined words. Practice listening to and saying the sentences with a partner.

It's a <u>BEAUtiful</u> day.   The <u>PRESident</u> is visiting today.

CD 2
Track 4

B Listen to this description of a person's neighborhood. Practice saying the sentences with a partner. Then answer the question.

One of the underlined words has a different stress pattern. Which one is it?

In my <u>neighborhood</u> there's a big <u>hospital</u> and a new <u>library</u>. A big movie <u>theater</u> is nearby. There's an <u>Internet</u> cafe on the first floor of my <u>apartment</u> building.

C Write a couple of sentences about your neighborhood. Use some of the underlined words in **B**. Read the sentences to a partner. Be careful of the word stress.

4 Speaking · **Is there a gas station near here?**

CD 2
Track 5

A Min Chul and Jan are driving to the movies. Look at the map and listen to their conversation. What are they looking for? Where is it?

Min Chul:	Uh-oh. I think we're running out of gas.
Jan:	OK . . . Where's the nearest gas station?
Min Chul:	I don't know. Let's ask someone.
Jan:	Excuse me.
Man:	Yes?
Jan:	Is there a gas station near here?
Man:	Yes. Go straight and turn right on Court Street. Go one block. It's on the corner of Court Street and First Avenue.
Jan:	Thanks!

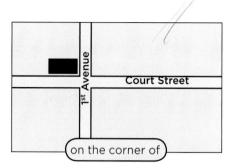

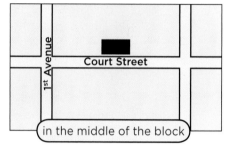

B Practice the conversation in groups of three.

5 Speaking Strategy

Useful Expressions
Asking for and giving directions

Asking about a specific place	Excuse me. Where's the Bridge Theater? It's **on** Jay Street. **Go straight** and **turn left** on Jay Street. It's **in the middle of the block**.
Asking about a place in general	Is there a gas station around here? Yes. **Go one block.** There's one **on the corner of** Court Street and First Avenue.

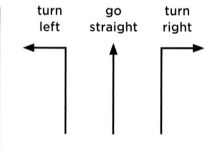

A Take turns asking a partner for directions to different places. Start at the **X**. Use the expressions in the box above.

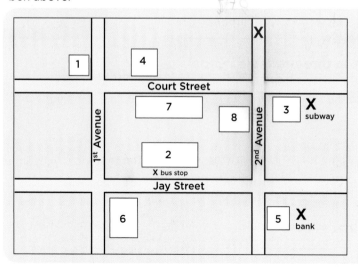

X Min Chul and Jan
1. gas station
2. Bridge Theater
3. Carl's Café
4. library
5. Pat's Hair Salon
6. grocery store
7. Jimmy's Gym
8. bookstore

B Choose one place in **A** and make a short conversation. You can use the conversation at the top of the page as a model. Perform it for the class.

6 Language Link   Prepositions of place

A Carla is a new student at Greenville College. Read part of Sidney's e-mail to Carla. Circle all the different places she describes. Then follow the instructions.

1. As you read the letter, notice the words in blue.

2. Work with a partner. Use the map on page 72 to find the places Sidney mentions.

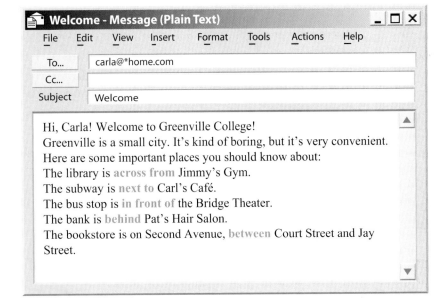

Welcome - Message (Plain Text)

File Edit View Insert Format Tools Actions Help

To...   carla@*home.com
Cc...
Subject   Welcome

Hi, Carla! Welcome to Greenville College!
Greenville is a small city. It's kind of boring, but it's very convenient.
Here are some important places you should know about:
The library is **across from** Jimmy's Gym.
The subway is **next to** Carl's Café.
The bus stop is **in front of** the Bridge Theater.
The bank is **behind** Pat's Hair Salon.
The bookstore is on Second Avenue, **between** Court Street and Jay Street.

B Look at the map and answer the questions.

1. What's in front of the Mexican restaurant?

    a bus stop

2. What's across from the theater?

    Coffe shop

3. What's behind the cafe?

    Nail Salon

4. What's next to the theater?

    mexican food

5. What's in front of the gym?

    news stand

6. What's between the gym and the bank?

    café shop

C Make a plan to meet at one of the places in **B**. Describe the location of the place.

A: Let's work out together at the gym.

B: Sounds good. When do you want to meet?

A: How about on Saturday at 2:00?

B: OK. Where's the gym exactly?

A: It's at . . .

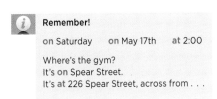

Remember!

on Saturday   on May 17th   at 2:00

Where's the gym?
It's on Spear Street.
It's at 226 Spear Street, across from . . .

7 Communication A death at 50 Dean Street

A Read the information. Then answer the questions below with a partner.

Miss Smith and Miss Jones live in the same apartment building at 50 Dean Street. They have tea together every Thursday afternoon at 4:00.

On this Thursday Miss Smith doesn't answer the doorbell. Miss Jones calls Mr. Busby, the apartment manager. He has a key to Miss Smith's apartment. He opens the door and sees Miss Smith on the floor. She is dead!

Later, the police find an apartment key under Miss Smith's sofa. The number on the key is 300. The key belongs to the killer.

- *Who are Miss Smith and Miss Jones?*

- *Who is Mr. Busby?*

- *What do Miss Jones and Mr. Busby see?*

- *What do the police find? Why is it important?*

The neighbors at 50 Dean Street

Miss Jones

Miss Smith

Mr./Mrs. Busby

Ms. Sanchez   Mr. Hu   Dr. Lewis

B Work with your partner to find the killer. Try to be the first in the class.

Partner A: Read the sentences to your partner.

Miss Smith lives in apartment 305.

Mr. and Mrs. Busby live across from Miss Smith.

Ms. Sanchez lives between Miss Jones and Mr. and Mrs. Busby.

Mr. Hu lives across from Ms. Sanchez.

The apartment next to Miss Smith's is 303.

Mr. Hu lives next to Dr. Lewis.

Dr. Lewis lives across from apartment 300.

Partner B: Write the names and room numbers below.

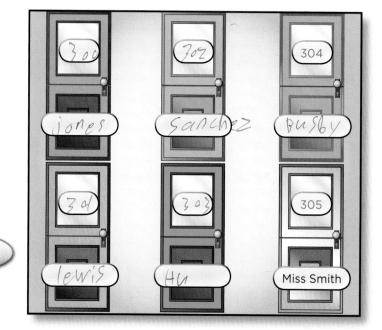

> Let's see. Miss Smith lives in Apartment 305.

> Miss Smith . . . 305 . . . OK, got it!

In the City

Lesson B Cities around the world

1 Vocabulary Link   What's your city like?

A Look at the photos and read the sentences. Pay attention to the words in blue.

It's easy to get **stuck in traffic** for hours.

There's **a lot of** pollution here.

The **weather** is hot and **humid** in the summer, but winters are very dry.

Public transportation is cheap. You can go anywhere for only two dollars.

B Read these sentences about different cities. Which statements are good qualities of places (**+**)? Which ones are not good (**–**)? Write "**+**" or "**–**".

pollution	1. There's a lot of pollution here. (**–**)
	2. It's pretty polluted here. (**–**)
	3. It's not very polluted at all. (**+**)
traffic	4. Traffic is heavy, especially during rush hour. (**–**)
	5. Traffic is light most of the time. (**+**)
	6. Overall, traffic flows pretty well. (**+**)
	7. You can get stuck in traffic for two hours or more. (**–**)
transportation	8. Public transportation is affordable. You can go anywhere for only two dollars. (**+**)
	9. There are many forms of transportation here: bicycles, cars, trains, and buses. (**+**)
weather	10. Winters are mild and summers are pleasant. It's very easy to live here. (**+**)
	11. The weather is severe in the winter: it's very cold and snowy. (**+**)
	12. Summers are hot and humid. It rains a lot. (**+**)

C Look at the sentences in **B**. Which ones describe your city or town?

There's a lot of pollution in my city.

Really? My city isn't very polluted at all.

2 Listening — Visit Vermont!

A Look at the photos. Which things do you enjoy? Tell a partner.

B Listen. Circle the correct answer to complete the sentence. Then put an X on the things in **A** that are NOT mentioned.

You are hearing **a news report / an advertisement**.

CD 2
Track 6

C Listen again and circle the correct word to complete each sentence.

1. Vermont is **polluted / quiet**.
2. The capital city has **heavy / light** traffic.
3. It's famous for **apples / oranges**.
4. It's a pretty **boring / interesting** place.

ASK ANSWER

Would you like to visit Vermont? Why or why not?

WORLD LINK

What's the highest capital city in the world?
a. La Paz, Bolivia
b. Kathmandu, Nepal
c. Bern, Switzerland

3 Reading — The best cities

A Look at the highlighted words in the reading. Which ones are count nouns? Which ones are noncount? Complete the chart.

Count nouns	Noncount nouns
rain forests	

B Look at the title of the reading. Why do you think San Jose and Hong Kong are two of the world's best cities? Tell a partner. Then read the passage to check your ideas.

C What do these articles say about San Jose and Hong Kong? Complete the chart. Write "NM" if the topic is not mentioned.

	San Jose, Costa Rica	Hong Kong, China
weather	San Jose has comfortable weather all year.	NM
housing		
transportation		
traffic		
parks		
food		

The Best Cities to Live in

SAN JOSE, COSTA RICA

When people think of Costa Rica, they imagine rain forests, rivers, and beautiful beaches. These things are not in San Jose. But this city is still one of the world's best. Why?

Unlike other cities in Central and South America, San Jose has comfortable weather all year (15°C/60°F to 26°C/79°F).

Housing is affordable in San Jose. Also, many of the city's older neighborhoods are very beautiful and have small hotels, art galleries, and cafes.

Beautiful volcanoes and mountains surround the city. You can visit them easily from San Jose.

One negative point: There's good public transportation, but heavy traffic is a problem in the city center.

HONG KONG, CHINA

Why live in Hong Kong? Here are two good reasons.

The city: This lively city—once a small fishing village—is today an international business center. It is an interesting mix of East and West, old and new. Modern skyscrapers are next to small temples. Popular nightclubs are close to traditional teahouses. Busy crowds fill the streets at all hours of the day. But outside the city, there are parks for walking or relaxing.

The food: Hong Kong is famous for its wonderful native dishes like dim sum. There's also food from Europe, North America, and other parts of Asia.

One negative point: Seven million people live in this small city! That's why housing is often very expensive.

ASK ANSWER

Which city are you interested in: San Jose or Hong Kong? Why?
What's important to you in a city? Check your answer(s) and explain your reasons.
_____ weather _____ safety _____ public transportation _____ nightlife

4 Language Link Questions and answers with *How much / How many*

A Study the chart of questions and answers about a city. Then circle the best answers to complete the three sentences.

How many is used with count nouns.	*How much* is used with noncount nouns.	Long and Short Answers
How many parks are there?	*How much pollution is there?*	*How many parks are there?*
There are **a lot**. / A lot.	There's **a lot**. / A lot.	There are a lot of parks.
There are **a few**. / A few.	There's **a little**. / A little.	There are a lot.
There are **two**. / Two.	_____	A lot.
There **aren't** many. / Not many.	There **isn't** much. / Not much.	
There **aren't** any. / None.	There **isn't** any. / None.	

1. Use *is / are* to answer questions with *how many*.

2. Use *is / are* to answer questions with *how much*.

3. You can use numbers (one, two, three, etc.) to answer questions with *how much / how many*.

B Choose the sentence closest in meaning to the underlined sentence.

1. <u>There isn't much traffic on this road.</u>

   a. The traffic is heavy.

   b. The traffic is light.

   c. There are no cars on the road.

2. <u>How much public transportation is available?</u>

   a. How many different kinds of public transportation are there?

   b. How much does transportation cost?

   c. How much traffic is there?

3. <u>There isn't much pollution in the air today.</u>

   a. It's very polluted.

   b. It's pretty polluted.

   c. It's not very polluted.

4. <u>There are some parks downtown.</u>

   a. There aren't many parks downtown.

   b. There are a few parks downtown.

   c. There are a lot of parks downtown.

5. <u>What's the population of your city?</u>

   a. How many people live in your city?

   b. How crowded is your city?

   c. Is your city very busy?

C Take turns asking and answering these questions with a partner.

1. How much homework did you do yesterday?

2. How many students are in class today?

3. How many days of school did you miss last month?

4. How much breakfast did you eat?

5. How many relatives do you have?

6. How much free time do you have on the weekend?

I missed three days of school last month.

5 Writing   **Creating a brochure**

> Every four years, the Summer Olympics are in a different city. Many cities compete to host the games.

A Read this brochure. This city wants to host the 2020 Summer Olympics. Does it sound like a good city?

Pleasant Valley
Wants to be the Next Host City for the 2020 Summer Olympics!

Pleasant Valley has very mild weather— over 300 days of sunshine a year!

There are many great neighborhoods in **Pleasant Valley**.

The Downtown Area is the center of business and excitement. There is a convenient subway system. It connects to an international airport.

The Northern District is famous for its hotels and restaurants.

South Beach has 20 kilometers of unpolluted beaches and a brand-new stadium.

B Imagine that your city wants to host the 2020 Summer Olympics. Make your own brochure with a partner.

1. Choose the information you want to put in your brochure:
   - the weather in my city/country
   - public transportation
   - hotels and restaurants
   - airports and train stations
   - traffic
   - amount of pollution
   - other idea: _____

2. Think about how to organize the brochure.
   - How will you present the information?
   - What pictures will you use?

Remember to be positive! The class will choose the best brochure to represent your city.

6 Communication   **Which brochure is best?**

A Present your brochures!

- **The Presenters:** With your partner, present your brochure to the class. Each person should explain a part of the brochure.

- **The Listeners:** For each presentation, complete these sentences:

I liked _____ about this brochure.

I wanted to hear more about _____.

B Look at your notes in **A**. Which brochure and presentation was the best? Why? Tell a partner.

C As a class, choose the best brochure.

 Check out the World Link video.   Practice your English online at http://elt.heinle.com/worldlink

1   Vocabulary Link   Sports and activities

A   Look at the list of activities. Each column is missing the same vowel (*a, e, i, o,* or *u*). Complete the missing letters. Then tell a partner: Which activities do you like? Which do you dislike?

1. b__seb__ll
2. b__sketb__ll
3. volleyb__ll
4. b__dminton
5. sw__mm__ng
6. p__ng pong
7. camp__ng
8. sk__ __ng
9. y__ga
10. jud__
11. b__wling
12. aer__bics
13. vid__o gam__s
14. t__nnis
15. socc__r
16. Pilat__s

B   The words in **A** are often used with the verbs *play*, *go*, and *do*. Complete the word webs below with the activities in **A**.

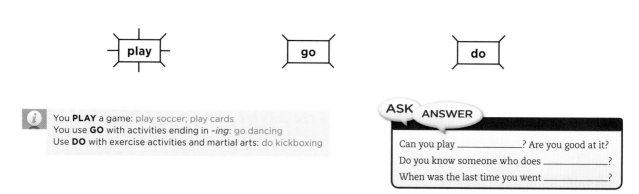

| play | go | do |

You **PLAY** a game: play soccer; play cards
You use **GO** with activities ending in *-ing*: go dancing
Use **DO** with exercise activities and martial arts: do kickboxing

ASK **ANSWER**

Can you play _____? Are you good at it?
Do you know someone who does _____?
When was the last time you went _____?

2 Listening **A different family**

> Imagine you can stop studying or working and follow your dream. What would you do?

 A Read the paragraph below. Then answer the question.

From Physician to Beach Bum

In the 1950s, Dorian "Doc" Paskowitz was a successful physician. He was handsome and in good health. To many people, Doc's life seemed perfect. But it wasn't. Doc was unhappy. He didn't like his work. The one thing he loved was surfing. So one day, Doc decided to change his life . . .

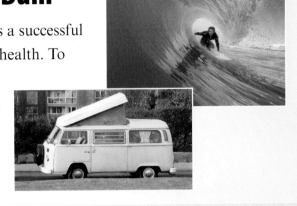

What do you think happened to Doc Paskowitz and his family? Circle your answers. (Use the photos as clues.) Then explain your ideas to a partner.

a. He surfed all the time.

b. He became a doctor in another city.

c. He traveled with his family.

d. He built a house on the beach.

 B Listen and check your answers in **A**.

CD 2
Track 7

 C Listen. Circle all the things that Doc and his family did.

CD 2
Track 8

1. Doc became sick.

2. He had a big family.

3. They visited many places.

4. They owned a business.

5. The children went to school.

6. The family was rich.

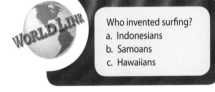

Who invented surfing?
a. Indonesians
b. Samoans
c. Hawaiians

ASK ANSWER

What do you think of the Paskowitz family? Did they have a good life? Why or why not?

3 Pronunciation **Reduced *to***

 A The pronunciation of *to* is usually reduced. Listen to these sentences. Notice the weak, short pronunciation of *to*.

CD 2
Track 9

1. I like to play golf.

2. She likes to go jogging.

3. I love to sleep late.

4. He hates to study.

5. We plan to fly to Paris.

6. Do you like to play chess?

7. I want to be early.

8. I hate to be late.

 B Practice saying the sentences in **A** with your partner. Pay attention to the pronunciation of *to*.

4 Speaking   **Do you want to play tennis?**

A Listen to the conversation. Underline Connie's offer. Circle Gina's invitation.

CD 2
Track 10

Connie: Hey, Gina. Do you want some ice cream?

Gina: No thanks. I'm going out.

Connie: Really? Where are you going?

Gina: I'm going to play tennis. Do you want to come?

Connie: Sorry, I can't. I need to study.

Gina: Well, come later then. We're playing all afternoon.

Connie: It sounds nice . . . But I'm not very good at tennis.

Gina: Don't worry about that. You don't have to play. You can just watch. Come on, it'll be fun.

Connie: Well, okay. I'll see you in an hour.

Gina: Ok, see you later. . . . And maybe we can have some ice cream afterwards!

B Practice the conversation with a partner.

5 Speaking Strategy

A Complete the information below.

1. Sport or activity I like to do: _Swimming_
2. Place to do it: _gym_
3. Day/time I want to do it: _weekend_

> **Notice**
>
> *want* + *to* + verb
> Do you want to play tennis tonight?
> *want* + noun
> Do you want a glass of water (or something)?

B Make a conversation. Use the dialog above and the Useful Expressions to help you. Follow the steps below.

1. Invite your partner to do your activity.
2. Your partner should first decline the invitation.
3. Next your partner accepts it.
4. Switch roles and do it again.

C Perform one of your conversations for the class.

Useful Expressions	
Do you want	
inviting	Do you want to come?
	Sure, I'd love to!
	Sorry, I can't. I'm busy.
	Um, no thanks. I'm not good at . . .
offering	Do you want some ice cream?
	Yes, please./Yes, thanks.
	No, thank you.
	No, thanks. I'm fine.

6 Language Link · Verb + noun; verb + infinitive

A Study the chart. Notice the verbs and the underlined words.

I love/like/hate/enjoy <u>sports</u>.	A noun or noun phrase can follow many verbs.
I love/like/learned <u>to play tennis</u>. I want/plan <u>to visit Australia</u> next year.	The infinitive can follow some verbs.

B Read the sentences. Underline the main verb. Is the main verb followed by a noun or noun phrase or by an infinitive? Write *N* (for noun or noun phrase) or *I* (for infinitive).

1. I <u>like</u> to swim. _____I_____
2. I don't like this video game. _____N_____
3. Diane wants a new swimsuit. _____N_____
4. Does he want to play tennis? _____I_____

5. They prefer to watch sports. _____I_____
6. We expect to win the game. _____I_____
7. I hate loud music. _____N_____
8. She decided to buy a yoga mat. _____I_____

C This is Jenna. For each picture, make up a sentence about her. Use the verbs in the boxes.

want

learn

love

not enjoy

decide

prefer

D Read your ideas to your partner. Are they the same?

> Jenna wanted to ski.

> You can also say Jenna wanted to go skiing.

7 Communication   **Who said that?**

A   Read the questions below. Write your answers under *My answer* in the chart.

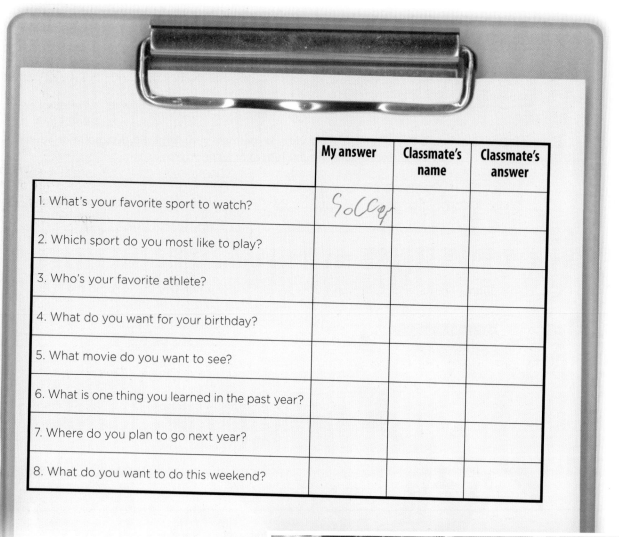

	My answer	Classmate's name	Classmate's answer
1. What's your favorite sport to watch?	Soccer		
2. Which sport do you most like to play?			
3. Who's your favorite athlete?			
4. What do you want for your birthday?			
5. What movie do you want to see?			
6. What is one thing you learned in the past year?			
7. Where do you plan to go next year?			
8. What do you want to do this weekend?			

B   For each question, interview a *different* classmate. Write each person's name and answer in the chart.

C   Join a group of three people. For each question, read a classmate's answer. Do *not* say the person's name. Your group guesses which classmate gave that answer.

> I asked the question "What's your favorite sport to watch?" This person loves to watch tennis.

> I know! That's Mateo.

> Yes, that's right!

All About You

Lesson B   What are you like?

1   Vocabulary Link   Terrific twins

A   Penny and Pearl are twins. Read about their personalities. Notice the words in **blue**. Which ones are opposites?

Penny and Pearl are friendly. They are also **bright** (intelligent).
However, their friends say they are very different.

Penny is very **organized**. She knows where everything is in her apartment.

Penny is pretty **ambitious**. Someday, she wants to be the CEO of her own company.

Penny's very **careful** with her money. In fact, she's a little bit **selfish**—sometimes she doesn't like to share.

Penny is somewhat **reserved**. She has two or three close friends and doesn't go out a lot.

Pearl's apartment is kind of **messy**: there are dirty dishes in the sink and magazines all over the floor.

Pearl enjoys her job and she has a very **laid back** (relaxed) attitude about life and work.

Sometimes Pearl is **careless** with money—she forgets to pay her bills on time.

She's very **generous**, though. She will share anything with you.

Pearl is **talkative**. She makes friends easily and is comfortable at parties.

B   Look at the pictures.

Which ones belong to Pearl? to Penny?

How do you know? Write their names.

> **i** **Notice!** You can use these words to weaken some personality adjectives:
>
> a little (bit) **selfish**   somewhat **reserved**   kind of **messy**

1. _____   2. _____   3. _____   4. _____

C   Look at these words from a dictionary. Which ones do you think describe Pearl? Which ones describe Penny? Explain your answers to a partner.

A **competitive** person wants to be more successful than other people.

An **impulsive** person does things suddenly without thinking carefully.

A **creative** person has a lot of new ideas, especially in the arts (music, dance, etc.).

A **private** person doesn't like others to know how he or she feels.

> **ASK ANSWER**
>
> Is your personality more like Pearl's or Penny's? How?
>
> There are several words on this page that end in –ive. What are they? Can you think of any more words?

2 Listening   Type A personality

A Look at the pictures and read the text with a partner. Answer the question.

"Type A" and "Type B" are two names experts use to describe personality. What do you know about these names? Which picture shows a Type A person?

CD 2
Track 11

B Listen. Circle the answer to complete each sentence.

1. This talk is happening at a _____.

   a. school   b. company   c. hospital

2. He is talking about the personality of _____.

   a. a student   b. a co-worker   c. people in general

> **ⓘ Notice these opposites.**
> possible ↔ impossible
> patient ↔ impatient
> perfect ↔ imperfect
> Practice saying these words.

CD 2
Track 11

C Listen again. Check all the words that describe the Type A person. Compare your answers with a partner.

❏ angry   ❏ laid back   ❏ patient

❏ competitive   ❏ nervous   ❏ a workaholic

ASK ANSWER

Are you more Type A or Type B? Why?

D The student says that Type B people are the opposite of Type A. What words describe Type B? Make a list of your ideas.

3 Reading   I'm a dreamer

A The reading on page 87 talks about four personality types. Before you read, follow these steps.

1. Look at the photos and read the list of famous names.

2. Choose one person and tell your partner about him or her. Where is the famous person from? What did he or she do?

3. Think of one more person to add to one of the lists. Explain your choice.

WORLD LINK

Type A and B personality theory was once used to predict:
a. heart attacks
b. strokes
c. cancer

B You have one minute. Scan the article. How many of these jobs can you find?

❏ actor   ❏ fashion designer   ❏ musician   ❏ scientist

❏ athlete   ❏ lawyer   ❏ police officer   ❏ teacher

❏ explorer   ❏ manager   ❏ politician   ❏ writer

C Circle the personality type for each statement. (Both answers are possible for one of the items.)

1. They like to follow rules.   The Partner / The Artist

2. They have strong ideas about things.   The Thinker / The Artist

3. They are more cheerful than serious.   The Artist / The Partner

4. They listen to other people's opinions.   The Dreamer / The Thinker

What is your personality type?

What is your personality type? Are you similar to Gandhi or Madonna? Queen Elizabeth or Socrates?
Read about these types and find out!

The Dreamer

A Dreamer thinks there is a "right" way to do things. This person wants to live in the "perfect world." A Dreamer is often hardworking and organized. Many are good listeners and like to help others. Many Dreamers work as teachers, lawyers, and in leadership roles.

Famous Dreamers: Mohandas Gandhi, Angelina Jolie, Aung San Suu Kyi

Angelina Jolie, actor and activist

Queen Elizabeth II

The Partner

A Partner wants to be in a group. For this person, rules and group harmony are important. They value tradition. Partners are often serious, careful people. Many do well as teachers, managers, police officers, and politicians.

Famous Partners: Queen Elizabeth II, Mother Teresa

The Thinker

For Thinkers, understanding things is very important. They like to solve problems and make new things. Thinkers can also be competitive. They like to win. They are independent and often have very strong opinions. Many Thinkers work as scientists, inventors, politicians, and engineers.

Famous Thinkers: Bill Gates, Socrates, Stephen Hawking

Stephen Hawking, scientist

Cristiano Ronaldo, athlete

The Artist

Artists want to be free. They don't want to follow the rules all the time. Artists like action and are often impulsive. They also like trying new things. Like Thinkers, many Artists have strong opinions. Many Artists are cheerful and creative and do well as musicians, actors, fashion designers, and athletes.

Famous Artists: Madonna, Cristiano Ronaldo

4 Language Link *How often…?; frequency expressions*

A Study the chart. Ask and answer the two questions with your partner.

| How often do you check email? | Every
Every other | day / Monday / week / month / year / summer. |
| | Once / Twice / Three times
Several times | a day / a week / a month / a year. |
| How often do you text your friends? | All the time. (= very often)
Once in a while. (= sometimes)
Hardly ever. (= almost never) | |

B Look at Ricardo's weekly schedule for the month of March. Answer each question. (Two answers are possible for items 1–3.)

How often does Ricardo…

1. have class? Three _____; every _____
2. work? every_____; _____
3. work from 3-6? _____; _____
4. meet with his study group? _____

Monday/9	Tuesday/10	Wednesday/11	Thursday/12	Friday/13	Saturday/14	Sunday/15
Class
9-12	Work
10-2	Class 9-12	Work 10-2	Class
9-12	Study group
10-12**	Work 3-6
Work 1-4		Work 1-4		Work 1-4	Work 1-4	
**Study group meets on March 14; next meeting April 13						

C Take turns asking and answering questions about these activities with a partner. Explain your answers.

go to English class   go on a date   go on vacation   get a haircut

go shopping   watch TV   exercise   take tests

> How often do you go to English class?

> Hardly ever.

> Really?

> No, I'm only joking. I go to English class three times a week. I also go to the language lab every other day.

5 Writing   **What are you like?**

A Choose three words from page 85 that describe your personality.

B Write about yourself. Use the three words and at least one of the words in the box.

> pretty   little   kind of   very

C Exchange your paper with a partner's. How are you similar? How are you different?

> You might think I'm kind of shy. Once you get to know me, I'm a pretty friendly person. I am also a little messy. I try to clean my room once a week, but I hardly ever do it!

6 Communication **Learn about yourself**

A Use the chart to interview a partner. Circle his or her answers.

Personality Quiz

Questions	Answers	
How often do you clean your room?	**a.** once a week	**b.** once in a while
How often do friends ask for your advice?	**a.** all the time	**b.** hardly ever
What is more important?	**a.** being kind	**b.** being honest
What is more important?	**a.** agreeing with the group	**b.** saying my opinion
Are you careful with money?	**a.** Yes, most of the time.	**b.** No, not really.
Which is important to you?	**a.** success	**b.** happiness
You're playing a game. Which sentence describes you?	**a.** I'm very competitive. I hate to lose.	**b.** I'm kind of laid back. I want to win, but if I lose, it's OK.
Your cell phone isn't working. What do you do?	**a.** try to fix it myself	**b.** ask for help
What is more important?	**a.** facts	**b.** feelings
What do you want in your life?	**a.** many different experiences	**b.** the same job
What is more important?	**a.** being free	**b.** being careful
You get a free ticket to Paris. The plane leaves tomorrow. Do you go?	**a.** Yes! I'm pretty impulsive.	**b.** No way! That's too scary.

B Total your partner's points for each color (a = 2 points, b = 1 point). Read about the color(s) with the *most* points on page 154, and tell your partner about his or her personality type(s).

C Do you agree with your description? Explain your opinion to your partner.

 Check out the World Link video.   Practice your English online at http://elt.heinle.com/worldlink

1   Vocabulary Link   Martin's new look

A   Look at the two pictures of Martin. How are they different?
Tell your partner one or two differences.

> In the first picture, Martin is working at home. In the second...

last year

this year

B   Look at the picture of Martin this year. His life has changed a lot.
Which sentences describe his changes? Circle the correct sentence.

1. Martin lost his job. / Martin found a new job.

2. He's making <u>more</u> money. / He's making <u>less</u> money.

3. He lost weight. / He gained weight.

4. He exercises a lot now. He's in good shape. / He's in bad shape.

5. He started smoking. / He stopped smoking.

> **ⓘ Notice!**
> Some verbs can be followed by verb + *-ing*:
>
> Let's <u>go</u> bowl**ing**!
> My dad <u>stopped</u> smok**ing**.
> I <u>enjoy</u> meet**ing** new people.

C   Look at the sentences below. Then find a similar sentence in **B**.

1. He's out of shape. = _____

2. He got a new job. = _____

3. He quit smoking. = _____

4. He's earning more money. = _____

> **ASK ANSWER**
>
> What do you want to do this year?
> Circle your answer(s). Tell a partner.
>
> get in shape   earn more money
> find a new job   start/quit _____
> other idea: _____

2 Listening **Another year is over**

 join = become a member
We can join many things:
a team, a club, a gym,
a band, the army

> What is one group or club you want to join? Why? Tell a partner.

A Many people make changes at the New Year. What is one change you tried to make in the past?

CD 2
Track 12

B Before you listen, read the sentences. Can you guess the answers? Then listen and complete the definition.

A New Year's resolution is a kind of personal _____ you make. You decide to make a _____ in the new year and work very _____ to do it.

CD 2
Track 13

C What are Jamal and Lea's resolutions? Write "J" for Jamal and "L" for Lea. (There are two extras.)

_____ 1. get better grades _____ 4. earn money

_____ 2. find a part-time job _____ 5. lose weight

_____ 3. join a gym _____ 6. gain weight

ASK ANSWER

Take turns. Tell a partner about Jamal and Lea's resolutions. Do you have any of the same goals?

3 Pronunciation **Contrastive stress**

CD 2
Track 14

A Listen to these short conversations. Notice the stress on the underlined words. Practice the conversations.

A: Is she making more money in her new job?

B: No, she's making <u>LESS</u> money.

A: How's your diet going? Did you lose weight or gain weight?

B: Unfortunately, I <u>GAINED</u> two kilos.

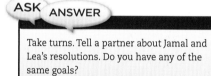 **Note:** Use stress for
—different information
—choices

CD 2
Track 15

B Look at these two conversations. Underline B's stressed words. Then listen and check your answers.

A: I heard that you got a ninety-five on your test.

B: No, actually, I got a hundred.

A: What kind of band did you join?

B: I joined a jazz band.

When is New Year's celebrated in China?
a. early December
b. early January but not January 1st
c. late January or early February

C Make a conversation with a partner. Give different information or respond to choices. Use proper stress.

4 Speaking — Can I borrow $20?

CD 2 Track 16

A Listen to the conversation. What does Zack want from Juan? How does he ask for it?

Zack: See you later, Juan. I'm going out for a while.

Juan: OK, see you.

Zack: Oh no!

Juan: What?

Zack: I forgot to go to the ATM.

Juan: Do you need money?

Zack: Yeah, I'd like to get a haircut this afternoon. Can I borrow $20?

Juan: Sure, here you go.

Zack: Thanks a lot.

B Practice the conversation with a partner.

5 Speaking Strategy

A Choose an item from the box. Ask to borrow it from your partner and give a reason. Use the Useful Expressions to help you create a conversation.

your partner's cell phone	your partner's car
some money	your idea: _____

> Wendy, could I borrow your cell phone for a minute? I need to call my mom.

Useful Expressions

Making and responding to requests

Can/Could I borrow your cell phone?
(= Is it OK if I borrow . . .)
Can/Could you lend me your cell phone?
(= Would you please lend . . .)

Positive responses	Negative response
Sure. No problem. Certainly.	I'm sorry, but . . . (+ reason).

> ℹ️ You can add *please* to requests with *you*:
> *It's hot in here. Can you please open the window?*
>
> *May I . . .* is more polite than *Can/Could I . . .*
> *May I borrow your pen for a second?*

B Change roles and create a new conversation.

6 Language Link · *Like to* vs. *would like to*

A Read the sentences. Notice the underlined words. Then answer the questions below with a partner.

 I'd = I would

a. I <u>like to</u> visit Australia.
My favorite place is Bondi Beach.

b. I'<u>d like to</u> visit Australia next summer.
I have to save some money!

Which sentence . . .

1. means *I enjoy visiting Australia*?   a   b
2. means *I want to visit Australia*?   a   b
3. talks about a future desire?   a   b

B Read the questions. Then circle the correct words to complete each answer.

1. What do you usually do on the weekend?
   I like to / I'd like to relax.

2. Why is Mike studying Japanese?
   He likes to / He'd like to learn languages.

3. Why are you studying for the TOEFL exam?
   I like to / I'd like to study in the United States.

4. What's your New Year's resolution?
   I like to / I'd like to get in shape.

5. How was your trip to Brazil?
   We loved it! *We like to / We'd like to* visit again.

6. Do your parents both work?
   Yes, but *they like to / they'd like to* retire soon.

C Write sentences about yourself. Use these topics and start each sentence with *I like to* or *I'd like to*.

1. your free time

   _____

2. after graduation

   _____

3. your favorite TV show

   _____

4. fun places to visit in your city

   _____

5. things to do next summer

   _____

6. changes in your life

   _____

D Take turns talking about your answers in **C** with a partner.

7 Communication Bad habits

A Look at the lists of bad habits and bad qualities below. Add one more idea to each list. Tell your partner.

BAD HABITS	BAD QUALITIES
I bite my nails.	I'm messy.
spend too much money.	lazy.
eat a lot of junk food.	late all the time.
talk on the phone too much.	careless with money.
watch too much TV.	too laid back.
your idea: _____	your idea: _____

B Look at the pictures with a partner. What bad habits and bad qualities do these people have?

C **Student A:** Imagine that you are the person in picture 1 above. First, tell your partner about your bad habits and bad qualities. Then tell your partner how you want to change. Ask your partner for advice.

Student B: Listen to your partner. Suggest ways that he or she can change.

A: I like to go shopping, but I spend too much money.

B: You should try to save some money—a little bit each month.

A: I'd like to save money, but I have a lot of bills. And I'm careless with money! What can I do?

B: Well, don't use your credit cards. It's . . .

D Switch roles and do another role play. Student B is the person in picture 2 above.

Change

Lesson B Plans and dreams

1 Vocabulary Link After I graduate

Take off has many different meanings. Read the sentences. Which usage can you find in A?

1) I took <u>some time</u> off between jobs.
2) Our flight took off an hour late.
3) It was a hot day. I took off <u>my jacket</u>.

A Maria, May, and Gregg are college seniors. What are their plans after graduation? Read their comments and answer the three questions.

1. Who is going to study more? ☐ Maria ☐ May ☐ Gregg
2. Who is going to work? ☐ Maria ☐ May ☐ Gregg
3. Who is not going to work or study? ☐ Maria ☐ May ☐ Gregg

Maria

We're getting ready (preparing) for graduation, but I'm worried. I applied for several jobs already, but so far . . . nothing. I hope I can get a full-time job soon.

May

I can't believe it. I'm about to graduate. I want to be a physician. It takes several years to become a doctor, so I need to study more.

Gregg

I'm tired of studying and looking for a job. I can't take it anymore! I just want to take it easy and relax. Maybe I'll take the summer off from job hunting and just travel.

B Complete these sentences. Use the correct form of the words in blue from **A**.

You can use *take* **+ a time expression** to talk about general and specific times:

It takes several years to become a doctor.
It takes eight hours to drive from San Francisco to L.A.

1. The new supermarket is ___*getting ready*___ for business. They're opening soon.
2. I'd like to _____ a ski instructor.
3. It _____ only 15 minutes to prepare this dish.
4. I was sick last Friday. I _____ a day _____ from work.
5. My new job is difficult. I _____ the stress.
6. I was _____ leave. Suddenly, the phone rang.
7. Joe _____ for a summer job last week.
8. Don't worry! Just _____ and relax!
9. Jorge is _____ for his trip. He's packing now.

C Ask and answer these questions with a partner.

1. How long does it take to graduate from a university? three years? four? more?
2. After graduation, what do university students in your country do?

   ☐ Take a month off and then apply for jobs   ☐ Take it easy for several months

   ☐ Get a job right away

3. What do you want to do after graduation?

2 Listening — A hot new singer

A Who is your favorite singer? What did he or she do in the last couple of months? Check the boxes.

☐ went on tour   ☐ appeared on TV

☐ recorded an album   ☐ your idea: _____

CD 2
Track 17

B Listen to the interview with Yeliz, a singer. Circle the correct words to complete the sentences.

1. Yeliz is in Los Angeles / Istanbul now. She lives in Istanbul / Scotland.

2. She rarely / often travels.

3. You can buy Yeliz's CD in two / a few months.

4. Her tour starts in two / six months. She'll visit two / six countries.

5. Yeliz will / won't quit singing in school.

CD 2
Track 17

C Listen again. How does Yeliz feel about these things? Circle your answers and write one key word that supports each answer.

How does Yeliz feel about · · · ·

1. traveling?   She likes / doesn't like it.   key word(s): _____

2. recording?   She likes / doesn't like it.   key word(s): _____

3. school?   She likes / doesn't like it.   key word(s): _____

> **ASK ANSWER**
> Do you think Yeliz's life is interesting? Why or why not?

3 Reading — A lifetime dream

A What is your dream job? Tell a partner. Why do you want to do it?

B Scan the article on page 97. Answer these two questions about Yi Wang and Hicham Nassir.

	Yi Wang	Hicham Nassir
What's her/his lifetime dream?		
What's stopping her/him?		

C Check "N" for what each person is doing now. Check "F" for their future plans. Underline a sentence in the reading that supports each answer.

Yi Wang

1. teach at a university ☐ N ☐ F

2. write a film ☐ N ☐ F

3. go to film festivals ☐ N ☐ F

Hicham Nassir

4. go to school ☐ N ☐ F

5. live in London ☐ N ☐ F

6. practice every day ☐ N ☐ F

> **ASK ANSWER**
> Think about your dream job again. What's stopping you from getting that job?

NEWS FROM A SMALL PLANET
A lifetime dream

This week, Jennifer Reece profiles the dreams of a Chinese professor and a Moroccan high school student.

"At the moment, I'm teaching chemistry at a university in Beijing. It's a good job, but my dream is to make films," says 29-year-old Yi Wang. "In China, young artists move to Beijing from all over the country. Many of them are painters, writers, and actors. I'd like to take some time off and make a film about their lives and their work."

Wang is writing a film now with help from her friends. But it isn't easy. "At the moment, the biggest problem is money," explains Wang. "We don't have much."

But this isn't going to stop Wang and her partners. "First, we're going to make this movie. Then, we'd like to show it in China, and maybe someday, at film festivals around the world."

Click here to read more....

Sixteen-year-old Hicham Nassir is getting ready for a soccer match with his teammates. Hicham, a student and his school's star player, is a native of Morocco. He now lives in London with his family.

"My parents want me to go to college and major in business or law," he explains. "They want me to get a job as a lawyer or work as a businessman. I understand them, but I want to become a pro soccer player. This summer, I'm going to practice really hard every day."

And what about his parents? "I hope they change their minds," says Hicham. "I want to play soccer professionally. It's my dream."

Click here to read more....

ASK ANSWER

Hicham Nassir's parents want him to go to college. Do your parents agree with your choices in life? Explain with an example.

4 Language Link   **The future with *be going to***

With a noun + *going to* we usually <u>say</u> the contraction = "My sister's going to take some time off."

But we <u>don't write</u> the contracted form: <u>My sister is</u> going to take some time off.

A   Study the chart. Then read about Neil and his family's summer plans. Complete his plans with the correct form of *be going to*.

subject + *be*		*going to* + verb		
I'm He's / She's You're /We're /They're	(not)	going to fly	to Mexico	this evening / this summer. next week / next month.

I _____ Japan after graduation. My brother _____
        (**1.** visit)   (**2.** stay)

home. He _____ anywhere. He _____ it easy.
            (**3.** not / travel)   (**4.** take)

My parents _____ a week off and going to the beach. We _____ all
                    (**5.** take)

_____ there in August. We _____ home until September 2.
        (**6.** meet)   (**7.** not / return)

B   Study the chart. Jo is asking Elliot about his trip around the world. Complete the dialog with *be going to*.

Yes/No questions	Are you going to work hard this summer?	Yes, I am. / Maybe. / No, I'm not.
Wh- questions	What are you going to do?	I'm going to take a trip.

Jo: So, (1. when / you / leave) _____ ?

Elliot: Next month.

Jo: (2. you / go) _____ with anyone?

Elliot: Yes, I am. (3. My roommate / come) _____ with me.

Jo: (4. Where / you / start) _____ the trip?

Elliot: First, (5. we / fly) _____ to London and spend a week there.

         Then (6. I / visit) _____ two more cities by myself.

Jo: Wow, how exciting. Send postcards!

C   Read these sentences with *be going to*. Each one has one error. Circle the letter of each error. Change the sentences to make them correct.

1. <u>Last</u> spring <u>I'm going to apply to</u> three <u>universities</u>.
   A   B   C   D

2. <u>My</u> family and I <u>am going to get</u> ready <u>at</u> 5:00.
   A   B   C   D

3. <u>Are</u> you <u>going to getting</u> a job <u>soon</u>?
   A   B   C   D

4. <u>The plane</u> is <u>going to not take off</u> <u>on time</u>.
   A   B   C   D

D   What are your plans for the weekend? Make a list. Ask and answer questions about your plans.

> What are you going to do this weekend?

> I'm going to hang out with my friends at a cafe.

5 Writing — My dream

A Read the paragraphs below. Then write about your dream. Don't write your name on your paper.

> My dream is to run in the Sao Paulo International Marathon. It's in June every year. I'm not going to run this year, but I'd like to enter next year.
>
> I think the marathon is going to be difficult. It's twenty-six miles! To prepare, I'm going to train for ten months. I know I'm not going to win the race. I just want to finish it!

 B Give your paper to your teacher. Your teacher gives you another student's paper. Read the paper you get. Guess the writer.

6 Communication — Plans for the future

A What are your plans for the near and distant future? Answer the questions in the chart. Then add one more.

Are you going to . . .	Yes, I am.	Maybe.	Probably not.	No, I'm not.
do something fun this weekend?				
continue to study English?				
take the TOEFL exam?				
move to another city?				
get married?				
have your own home?				
visit another country?				
learn another language?				
start your own business?				
_____ ?				

 B Take turns asking and answering the yes/no questions in **A** with a partner.

A: Are you going to move to another city?	A: Are you going to move to another city?
B: Yes, I am.	B: Probably not.
A: Really? Where are you going to move to?	A: Why not?
B: Toronto.	B: I like my hometown. It's comfortable here.

 Check out the World Link video.   Practice your English online at http://elt.heinle.com/worldlink

1 Storyboard

A Rolf is telling Brigit about his trip. Look at the pictures and complete the conversation. More than one answer may be possible for each blank.

B Practice the conversation. Then change roles and practice again.

2 See It and Say It

 A Talk about the picture.

- Where are these people?

- What are they doing?

- Look at the different ads. What are they about?

- How is the traffic and pollution in your city?

- How often do you take public transportation?
  What other forms of transportation do you take?

- Ask one more question about the picture.

B Choose one pair of people in the picture. Role play a conversation between the two people.

3 They're Going to Get Married!

A Look at the wedding announcement below. Two people are getting married. Think of a man and a woman. They can be famous people or other people you know. Complete the information about them.

We're Getting Married!

Name: _____ Name: _____

Occupation: _____ Occupation: _____

Age: _____ Age: _____

Where from: _____ Where from: _____

B Work alone. You are going to interview these people. Look at the questions and think of three more to ask the couple.

- When did you meet?
- How did you meet?
- When are you going to get married?
- Who are you going to invite to the wedding?
- Where _____ ?
- How much _____ ?
- _____ ?

C Conduct the interview.

Partner A: You are one of the people in **A.** Answer the reporter's questions. Use your imagination.

Partner B: You are a newspaper reporter. Use your questions to interview the man or woman. Take notes.

D Switch roles and do the interview again.

E Share some of your interview notes with another pair.

> I interviewed Justin Timberlake. He's dating Mia, our classmate! They're going to get married next month!

> Really? How did they meet?

4 Listening

CD 2
Track 18

Look at each photograph. Then listen to the four sentences for each.
Circle the letter of the sentence that best describes the photograph.

1.

    A   B   C   D

2.

    A   B   C   D

3.

    A   B   C   D

4.

    A   B   C   D

10 Your Health

Lesson A   The body

1   Vocabulary Link   Our bodies

 A   Watch your teacher say and point out these words. Then complete the diagram below. Practice saying the words.

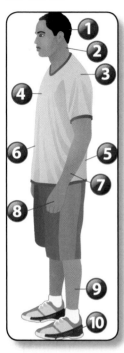

arm	_____	head	1
back	_____	leg	_____
chest	_____	neck	_____
foot	_____	shoulder	_____
hand	_____	stomach	_____

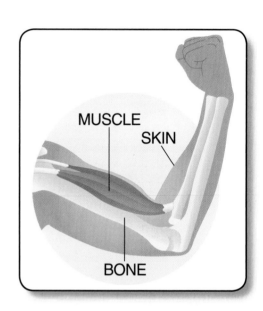

MUSCLE   SKIN

BONE

 B   Look at these words. Which adjectives are used to describe these parts of the body? Fill in the chart.

broad
long
muscular
narrow
short
strong

PARTS OF THE BODY			
arms	legs	neck	shoulders

 C   Look at the picture of Michael Phelps. First use the words in **A** to identify parts of the body. Then use the words in **B** to describe Michael.

He has strong legs.

2 Listening   **There's a stranger in my house!**

A In the U.S., people call 911 in an emergency (such as a fire, or a car accident). In your country, what phone number do you call? Have you ever called this number?

B In the picture, what is the woman doing? Tell a partner. Then listen and complete the sentences below.

CD 2 Track 19

The woman called _____ because she was _____ .

She saw a strange _____ in her _____ .

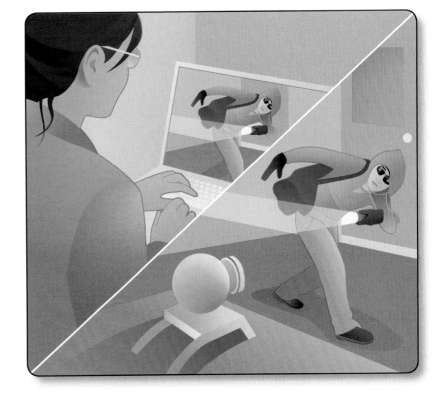

C Listen again. Circle the correct picture of the man. Who is the man?

CD 2
Track 19

3 Pronunciation   **Vowel shifts in plural forms**

A All of these nouns have irregular plural forms. Listen to how the vowel sound changes, and repeat.

CD 2
Track 20

tooth—teeth   foot—feet   man—men   woman—women   child—children

B Practice saying these sentences. Then listen and repeat.

CD 2
Track 21

1 a. My tooth hurts.
  b. My teeth hurt.

2 a. My foot is tired.
  b. My feet are tired.

3 a. The man is here.
  b. The men are here.

4 a. The woman is nice.
  b. The women are nice.

UNIT 10 • Your Health   105

4 Speaking **I don't feel well.**

CD 2
Track 22

A Listen to the conversation. What's wrong with Jon?
Check the boxes.

☐ His head hurts.   ☐ His back hurts.   ☐ He's tired.

Mia: Hello?

Jon: Hi, Mia. It's Jon.

Mia: Jon! Where are you? It's 7:30.
The movie starts in twenty minutes.

Jon: Sorry to call so late, but I can't meet you tonight.

Mia: Really?

Jon: Yeah, I don't feel well.

Mia: What's wrong?

Jon: I have a headache, and I'm really tired.

Mia: Oh, sorry to hear that. Well, get some rest, and
I'll call you in the morning.

Jon: OK. Talk to you then.

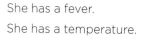

B Practice the conversation with a partner.

5 Speaking Strategy

A What's wrong with Jenna? Match each pair of sentences to one picture.

She has a backache.   She has a stomachache.   She has a sore throat.   She has a fever.
Her back hurts.   Her stomach hurts.   Her throat hurts.   She has a temperature.

B Take turns practicing the conversation in Speaking again. Use
the words you just learned in **A** to make a new conversation.

C Role play. You have plans to meet a friend, but you don't feel
well. Call your friend and explain the situation. Use the
Useful Expressions to help you.

D Change roles and practice again.

> Hi, Maria. It's Vince. Sorry,
> but I don't feel well.

> Oh, no! What's the
> matter?

Useful Expressions
Talking about health problems
What's wrong? / What's the matter?
I don't feel well.
I'm sick.
I have a/an . . .
My . . . hurts.

6 Language Link   Imperatives

A   Tom was stressed and didn't feel well. He went to see his doctor for advice.

- Read the sentences in the box.

- Choose the correct words to complete the doctor's advice.

1. Take / Don't take

2. Work / Don't work

3. Take / Don't take

4. drive / don't drive

> **Use the imperative to give orders, instructions, and warnings. Add *please* to make a request.**
>
> **1.** You're tired. _____ time to relax.
>
> **2.** _____ so hard.
>
> **3.** You need this medicine. _____ three pills twice a day.
>
> **4.** Please _____ when you take this medicine.

B   Read the information about unit nouns. Then complete the following health tips, using positive or negative imperatives. Use the verbs in the box.

> **Unit Nouns:**
> Use *a piece / a bit / a cup / a glass + of* to make noncount nouns countable.
>
> It's OK to have **a piece of cake** once in a while. Just don't eat too much.
>
> I always have **a cup of coffee** with breakfast.

| drink   eat   give   go   sleep   take   wash |

Health tips: The common cold	
To stay healthy:	**If you have a cold:**
1. ___*Take*___ vitamins.	**6.** _____ to school or work.
2. ___*Don't eat*___ a lot of junk food.	**7.** _____ too many cans of soda. Water is better.
3. _____ for 8–9 hours a night.	**8.** _____ an aspirin for pain and fever.
4. _____ your hands often.	**9.** _____ aspirin to children under 12! It's dangerous.
5. _____ a cup of green tea daily.	**10.** _____ a bowl of chicken soup.

C   Take turns with your partner. Imagine that you have one of these health problems. Add one more to the list. Ask your partner for some advice.

1. I can't sleep at night.

2. I have a stomachache.

3. When I go running, my legs hurt.

4. _____

> I can't sleep at night.

> Don't drink coffee in the evening!

7 Communication   Health posters

 A This poster gives advice. Read it and then answer the questions.

1. Where do you see posters like this in your city?

2. What does the poster tell people to do?

3. What other ideas can you add to the list?

Say **NO** to smoking.

Stop smoking today.
How can you do it?

- **Choose a date to stop smoking.**
- **Tell your friends and family about your plan.**
- **Talk to your doctor. Ask for help.**

 B Read the ideas for poster titles. With a partner, write another idea.

Fight pollution in our city!	Eat healthy, live longer.
Get in shape today!	Protect your skin this summer!
Don't drink and drive.	Your idea: _____

 C Write one of the poster titles from **B** in the chart. Think of how people can do it. List three ideas in the chart. On a separate piece of paper, make a poster using these ideas.

Poster Title: _____

How can you do it?

1. _____

2. _____

3. _____

 D Take turns presenting your poster to another pair. Discuss it with them. What do you like most about the poster? What is one piece of advice you would add to the poster?

Your Health

Lesson B Energy and stress

1 Vocabulary Link   I'm stressed.

A Read about these students' problems and match the advice (1 or 2) below with the correct person. Then practice asking for and giving the advice with a partner.

> I feel really stressed. Today is Wednesday and I have two papers due —one on Thursday and one on Friday! I always wait until the last minute to do homework.

Vicki

Lateef

> I work 60 hours a week. I'm under a lot of pressure to make money. In the past, I was always full of energy. But now, on the weekends, I'm so low on energy I just sleep all day. Help!

Take my advice . . .

1. Your situation is really stressful. But there are things you can do to reduce the stress. For example, try to work only 40-45 hours a week. Then you can relax—and you'll have more energy.

2. You don't have time to finish the papers now. Try to be calm. To deal with your problem now, talk to your teachers about it. Maybe they'll give you more time. In the future, try to plan better!

 Word partnerships

deal with stress, problems
reduce stress

full of energy
low on energy

Notice!
have (a lot of) energy
have time
but
feel stressed

B Answer the questions. Explain your answers with an example.

1. Do you wait until the last minute to do homework or study?

2. In the morning, are you usually full of energy or low on energy?

3. When are you under a lot of pressure at school or work?

4. In what way is speaking English stressful for you? How can you reduce the stress?

2 Listening **Now I'm full of energy!**

A Discuss this question with a partner.

What kinds of products do you buy when you . . .

are out of shape?   have low energy?   are feeling stressed?

CD 2
Track 23

B Listen. What is the advertisement about? Circle the picture.

 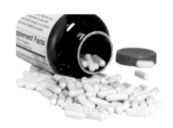  

CD 2
Track 24

C Listen. Complete each sentence with the missing information.
Are the sentences facts or opinions? Write "F" for fact, and "O" for opinion.

1. ___ The company was started in _____ .

2. ___ Each bottle has everything you need for a _____ life.

3. ___ You will _____ the vitamins.

4. ___ Each bottle costs _____ .

CD 2
Track 24

D Listen again and circle each word in the pair that you hear.
Then match the word to what it describes.

1. healthy / unhealthy   a. customer

2. happy / unhappy   b. life

3. happy / unhappy

4. lucky / unlucky

> **Opposites**
> happy → **un**happy
> healthy → **un**healthy
> lucky → **un**lucky

3 Reading **Exam prep**

A Read the message from *Sleepless in Seoul* on page 111. What is the writer's problem?

a. The writer is unhappy about her/his grade.

b. The writer is worried about a test.

c. The writer failed an exam last Friday.

B Read Donna's answer. At the beginning of each tip from Donna, write the correct introductory
sentence from this box.

> Eat well.   Take breaks and relax.   Get a study partner.   Don't do too much.

Dear Donna

Problems? Just ask Donna.

home | topics | archives

Advice Column

Archives

Email Donna

Dear Donna,
Help! I'm an 18-year-old high school student in Seoul. In eight months,
I'm going to take the university entrance exam. To prepare, I'm studying
six hours a day. I want to do well, but I'm really stressed these days.
I can't sleep. What can I do?

Signed,
Sleepless in Seoul

Dear Sleepless,
Your problem is a common one for many students around the world.
Here are some tips to help you deal with the stress. Good luck!

1. _____ Make a study schedule for yourself, but don't
study too much in one day. You remember more by studying one hour each
day for six days, than six hours in one day. Also, don't study late at night
(we often forget information studied then).

2. _____ You learn best when you study in two-hour blocks.
Every two hours, take a break for 15 to 20 minutes. Go outside and walk.
Exercise is a great way to reduce stress.

3. _____ Don't eat a lot of sugar or drink a lot of caffeine.
Eat foods high in vitamin B (for example, eggs, yogurt, green vegetables,
tofu, and rice). These give you energy and help you think more clearly.

4. _____ A study partner can help you practice for the test.
When you're worried about the exam, you can talk to your partner. This can
reduce stress, too.

C Check the sentences that you think Donna would agree with. Explain your answers to a partner.

1. ☐ It's better to study a little bit each day.

2. ☐ The best hours for studying are from 11 p.m. to 1 a.m.

3. ☐ Take a break but don't go outside. You need to focus.

4. ☐ Drink several cups of coffee to stay awake.

5. ☐ It's good to tell a study partner your feelings.

ASK ANSWER

What do you think of Donna's advice? Do you agree or disagree?
What was the last test you took? Was it hard? How did you prepare?

4 Language Link   *When* clauses

A   Study the sentences in the chart.

> The result can also come first in a sentence:
> I cry when I see sad movies.

When clause	Result clause	
When(ever) I drink a lot of coffee, When(ever) I see sad movies,	I can't sleep. I cry.	These sentences mean *When X happens, Y is the result.*

B   Match a *when*-clause on the left with a result clause on the right to make sentences.

1. When I feel stressed,
2. When we argue,
3. When I sleep well,
4. When I don't eat breakfast,
5. When you're kind,
6. When I miss the bus,

   a. people are usually nice to you.
   b. I get hungry by 10:00.
   c. my mom usually apologizes first.
   d. I exercise.
   e. I'm late for class.
   f. I have a lot of energy the next day.

C   Rewrite the sentences in **B** so that the result is first. Then tell your partner which sentences are true for you. Explain your answers.

1. *I exercise when I feel stressed.* _____
2. _____
3. _____
4. _____
5. _____
6. _____

D   Complete the sentences with your own information.

1. When I don't feel well, *I take aspirin and drink tea.* _____
2. When I meet new people, _____
3. When I don't understand something in English, _____
4. I feel stressed when _____
5. I feel _____ when _____

E   Take turns saying the sentences in **D**. For each sentence, your partner asks you one question.

5 Writing **A remedy for stress**

A When you feel stressed, what do you do? Read the paragraph about Dmitri. Then write your ideas on a separate piece of paper.

I'm a college senior. Next semester, I'm going to graduate. A lot of things in my life are going to change. Sometimes, I feel stressed. What do I do? I try to be calm. Whenever I'm under a lot of pressure, I talk to my friend Sergei. We talk about our future plans and I always feel better.

–Dmitri, Moscow

B Exchange your paper with a partner. Ask questions about your partner's ideas.

6 Communication **Stress survey**

A Interview your partner. Check (✔) the answer that describes him or her.

> **Stress Survey** _____
>
> 1. When you have to wait in a line, do you usually
>   - ❏ get nervous and impatient?
>   - ❏ wait patiently?
>   - ❏ other: _____
>
> 2. When you have a lot to do, do you usually
>   - ❏ wait until the last minute to do it?
>   - ❏ do a little bit every day?
>   - ❏ other: _____
>
> 3. When you have some free time, do you usually
>   - ❏ find something to do?
>   - ❏ relax?
>   - ❏ other: _____
>
> 4. When you feel stressed, what do you do?
>   - ❏ I don't tell anyone.
>   - ❏ I tell a friend or family member.
>   - ❏ other: _____
>
> 5. When someone disagrees with you, do you
>   - ❏ argue with the person?
>   - ❏ change your opinion?
>   - ❏ other: _____
>
> 6. What do you do when you're low on energy?
>   - ❏ I eat something.
>   - ❏ I take a nap.
>   - ❏ other: _____

B Think about your partner's answers. Is your partner a calm or a stressed person? Explain your answer.

Check out the World Link video.

Practice your English online at http://elt.heinle.com/worldlink

1 Vocabulary Link Never give up!

A Read this biography of Charice Pempengco. Then put the events in the correct order.

> Both talent and ability are nouns.
> *Notice!* Talent is also often used as an adjective: talent show, talent search, talent scout

___1___ appeared on *Little Big Star*

___3___ appeared on *Star King*

___4___ crowd loved her

___6___ entered many contests

___2___ got third place

___5___ sang with Celine Dion

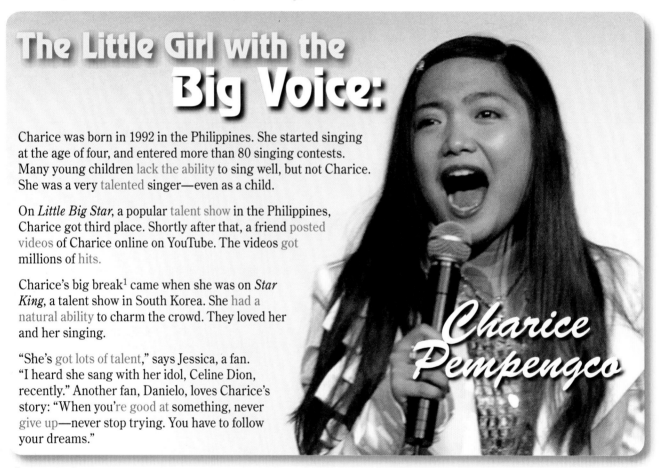

The Little Girl with the Big Voice:

Charice was born in 1992 in the Philippines. She started singing at the age of four, and entered more than 80 singing contests. Many young children lack the ability to sing well, but not Charice. She was a very talented singer—even as a child.

On *Little Big Star*, a popular talent show in the Philippines, Charice got third place. Shortly after that, a friend posted videos of Charice online on YouTube. The videos got millions of hits.

Charice's big break[1] came when she was on *Star King*, a talent show in South Korea. She had a natural ability to charm the crowd. They loved her and her singing.

"She's got lots of talent," says Jessica, a fan. "I heard she sang with her idol, Celine Dion, recently." Another fan, Danielo, loves Charice's story: "When you're good at something, never give up—never stop trying. You have to follow your dreams."

Charice Pempengco

[1]big break = big opportunity

B Complete sentences 1–5 with either *sing* or *singing*. Which sentences are similar in meaning?

1. She's really good at _____ .

2. He's terrible at _____ .

3. She has the ability to _____ really well.

4. He lacks the ability to _____ at all.

5. She was disappointed, but didn't give up _____ .

> **ASK ANSWER**
>
> In your opinion, who is the most talented singer today?
> Can you name a popular online video? How many hits did it get?
> What is something you're good at doing? What is something you're terrible at doing?

2 Listening **Good luck on your audition!**

A Look at these pictures. You are going to hear an interview. What do you think the interview is going to be about?

B Listen to the first part of the interview. Where is the interview taking place? Circle the appropriate picture in **A**.

C Listen to the complete interview. When do these events happen? Put them in order.

_____6_____ appear on TV

_____5_____ audition

_____2_____ check in

_____3_____ get a wristband

_____4_____ return tomorrow

_____1_____ wait for about two hours

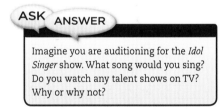

> ⓘ *audition* = a short performance given to show singing or acting ability

ASK ANSWER

Imagine you are auditioning for the *Idol Singer* show. What song would you sing? Do you watch any talent shows on TV? Why or why not?

3 Pronunciation *Can / can't*

A Listen to the sentences. Pay attention to the pronunciation of the underlined words.

1. She <u>can</u> speak three languages.
2. I <u>can't</u> play the piano.

B Listen and circle the word you hear.

1. Billy can / can't sing very well.

2. I can / can't do magic tricks.

3. I can / can't go out with you tonight.

4. Jill can / can't meet us after class.

C Say the sentences in **B** to your partner. Are you saying *can* or *can't*? Your partner points to the word.

4 Speaking   **You can paint really well.**

CD 2
Track 29

A Tyler and Ayumi are at a party. Listen to the conversation. Does Tyler like Ayumi's painting?

Ayumi: Hi, Tyler. Are you enjoying yourself?

Tyler: Yeah, I really am. What a great art show.

Ayumi: Yeah, it's really interesting.

Tyler: So . . . which painting is yours?

Ayumi: This one . . . right over here.

Tyler: Wow. I like it a lot.

Ayumi: Really? Thank you.

Tyler: How long did it take you to finish it?

Ayumi: About two months.

B Practice the conversation with a partner.

5 Speaking Strategy

A Read the Useful Expressions and responses. With a partner, write one follow-up question for each compliment and response.

Useful Expressions		
Offering compliments about things	**Responses**	**Follow-up questions**
Nice haircut!		Where did you get it done?
Cool glasses!		Were they expensive?
This is / That's an interesting story.	Thanks!	_____
I like your jacket a lot.	Thank you.	_____
What a great painting!	That's nice of you to say.	_____
Offering compliments about abilities		
You can speak English really well!		_____

B With a partner, create new conversations for Situations 1 and 2 below. Offer a compliment and ask follow-up questions.

Situation 1

Student A: You're a guitarist. You wrote a new song and you're practicing it.
Student B: You hear your partner practicing a song. You like it. You think your partner plays well.

Situation 2

Student B: You're wearing a new sweater. It didn't cost a lot of money.
Student A: Your partner is wearing a new sweater. You think it's cool.

6 Language Link   **Talking about talents with *can* and *know how to***

I **can** see better with my new glasses.
Not: I~~know how to see better with my new glasses.~~

A   Study the chart. Then complete the sentences below with the correct form of *can* or *know how to*. In which sentences are both possible?

Present	Past
Naoki can play the guitar. Naoki can't play the guitar.	Monika could read at age two. Monika couldn't read at age two.
Naoki knows how to play the guitar. Naoki doesn't know how to play the guitar.	Monika knew how to read at age two. Monika didn't know how to read at age two.

1. Jared is a language wiz. He _____ speak five languages fluently.

2. Jim was a very tall child. By the time he was eight, he _____ reach the top shelf in his kitchen.

3. Satoshi Fukushima _____ see or hear but he is still a successful professor at Tokyo University.

4. Valentina _____ count to 100 when she was three.

5. I'm going to post some videos online so I _____ watch them anytime I want.

6. For years, my grandmother _____ use a computer. Then she took a class. Now she _____ send e-mail, surf the Web, and shop online.

B   Add your own question to the chart. Then follow the steps below.

• Find a classmate who answers *Yes* for each question.

• Write the classmate's name.

• Ask the classmate to perform the action for you.

Can you . . . / Do you know how to . . .	Classmate's name
1. sing a song in English?	_____
2. draw a picture with your eyes closed?	_____
3. dance?	_____
4. say "I love you" in three languages?	_____
5. _____	_____

> Can you sing a song in English?

> Yes. I can sing "Happy Birthday."

ASK ANSWER

What is something you can do now but couldn't do in the past? How did you learn to do it?

7 Communication   *Talent Search!*

A   Read about the TV show *Talent Search!*
Do you know any other shows like this one?

> *Talent Search!* is a popular TV show. Talented people
> compete against each other for prizes. Some people
> sing or dance. Others tell jokes, do magic tricks, or
> act. The audience chooses the best person.

B   Imagine that you are going to be on *Talent Search!* Complete the form about yourself.

1. Name: _____

2. Where from: _____

3. What's your special talent? _____

4. What exactly are you going to do on the show? _____

C   Get together with a partner and ask him or her questions to complete the form in **B**. Write the answers on a separate piece of paper.

> **What's your special talent?**

> **Well, I can dance and sing in English . . .**

D   You and your partner should join two other pairs. Imagine that you are a *Talent Search!* announcer. Introduce your partner to the group. Use your notes from **C**.

E   Who has the most interesting talent in your group? Why?

That's Amazing!

Lesson B A sense of achievement

1   Vocabulary Link **Are you a risk-taker?**

A   Look at the pictures. Which one do you want to try? Why?

race car driving

living in a foreign country

opening a restaurant

B   Do you take risks in your life? Read through the survey once.
Then interview a partner.

> *A* risk-taker *is a person who is not afraid to try new things.*

Are you a **risk-taker?**

1. You want to open a restaurant, but you have to borrow a lot of money to reach your goal.
   Do you borrow the money?
   > Yes. I know I can do it.
   > No, it's too risky.

2. You have a chance to live in a foreign country for one month. The people there speak a different
   language so it will be hard to communicate. Do you go?
   > Yes, I like new experiences. I'm going to accept the challenge.
   > No, I would play it safe and stay home.

3. You are on a game show. You just won a lot of money. You can stop or answer one more question
   correctly and double your money. Do you take a chance and try the final question?
   > Yes, I'm a gambler.
   > No, I would stop.

4. You can go one lap (round) in a high-speed race car. Do you try it?
   > Yes, I'm pretty adventurous.
   > No, it's too dangerous.

5. You are working long hours in your job. You hate the job. Do you quit the job immediately?
   > Yes. I have a good chance of finding a new job very soon.
   > No. I keep working. At the same time, I look for a new job.

C   Is your partner an adventurous person? Does
he or she take a lot of chances or usually play it
safe? Present your partner to the class.

> Many adjectives end in *-ous.* How many of
> these words do you already know?
> | | |
> |---|---|
> | adventurous | dangerous |
> | ambitious | famous |
> | curious | nervous |

ng   What a show!

*Unit 11
Quiz
Dictation*

the amazing thing the man is going to talk about?
Circle your answers.

~~fs~~ / divers he saw in Mexico City / Acapulco.

CD 2
Track 31

B   Listen. What did the man do and see on his trip? Circle your answer(s).

1

2

3

4

cliffs

C   Why is cliff diving dangerous? Explain to your partner in your own words.

ASK   ANSWER

Many tourists visit La Quebrada to see the divers. Name a popular tourist attraction you know.

3   Reading   Two amazing achievements

A   Look at the headlines and pictures in the two articles on page 121. Try to answer the questions.

What does the girl do?   What did the boy do?

B   Now read the articles and check your answers. Did you guess correctly?

C   Scan each reading.

1. Find a word on line 12 that means "private teacher." _____

2. Find a word on line 15 that means "easy." _____

3. Find the word on line 19 that means "healthy." _____

4. Find a word on line 23 that means "a safe place for ships near land." _____

5. Find the words on line 29 that mean "the best part." _____

6. Find a word on line 30 that means "scary." _____

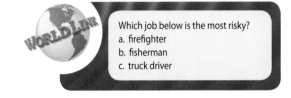

WORLD LINK

Which job below is the most risky?
a. firefighter
b. fisherman
c. truck driver

STAR of the SHOW

Natasha Patterson is only 11 years old. She weighs just 31 kilos. In many ways, Natasha looks like your typical "pre-teen." Don't let her appearance fool you.

Natasha travels the world with Cirque du Soleil,
5 an entertainment company from Montreal. The circus performs all over the world.

Natasha started gymnastics training when she was two years old. A couple of years ago, she auditioned for Cirque du Soleil. They gave her a job!

10 Now Natasha performs ten shows a week as a contortionist[1] in a Cirque du Soleil show. She travels with her mother and her brother, so a tutor teaches her while she is away from school. Natasha's father stays at home.

Natasha's work is a little bit dangerous. How did she learn
15 to do it? First, she started with simple tricks. Gradually, she started taking more risks.

Natasha's mother says it well: "Traveling all the time as a family is challenging. I have to make sure Natasha eats a nutritious diet and does her homework. But Natasha is happy . . .
20 so I'm happy too!"

[1] A contortionist can move his or her body into unusual positions.

A Sailing Success Story

Fifteen-year-old Sebastian Clover arrived in Antigua early yesterday morning. Clover, a high school student from the UK, sailed alone across the Atlantic Ocean. Waiting to meet him at the harbor were his parents, a band of musicians, and the Governor-General of
25 Antigua and Barbuda.

Sebastian's journey began on December 19. He sailed his boat from the Canary Islands and arrived in Antigua and Barbuda on January 12.

How was the trip? For Clover, the high point was seeing
30 whales and dolphins. But sometimes it was frightening being alone on the boat—especially in bad weather. It was also hard to eat well. Clover usually ate snacks because it was difficult to cook.

It was an amazing trip, but Sebastian also admits he's glad to be back on land!

D Who is each phrase about? Circle Natasha or Sebastian.

1. does gymnastics	Natasha	Sebastian
2. a high school student	Natasha	Sebastian
3. travels with other family members	Natasha	Sebastian
4. happy to be home	Natasha	Sebastian
5. eats well	Natasha	Sebastian

ASK ANSWER

Natasha and Sebastian had the chance to do something exciting. What is something adventurous you want to try?

4 Language Link   *Because* and *so*

A Study the sentences in the chart. Then complete the sentences below about Sebastian's sailing trip. (See page 121.)

Main clause	Reason
Natasha can't go to school	because she has a job.

Main clause	Result
Natasha can't go to school,	so she has a private tutor.

i The reason can also come first in a sentence: Because she has a job, Natasha doesn't go to school.

i Use *so* to show a result.

1. Because Sebastian likes a challenge, _____

2. It was difficult to cook, so _____

B Combine the sentences below using *because* or *so.*

1. The teacher is sick. There's no class today.

   _____

   _____

2. It was cold. We didn't go to the beach.

   _____

   _____

3. I had a headache. I took some aspirin.

   _____

   _____

4. School is closed for a month. We're going to take a trip.

   _____

   _____

C Circle *because* or *so.*

1. We didn't have the picnic because / so it was raining.

2. I felt confident, because / so I decided to accept the challenge.

3. I don't gamble because / so it's too risky.

4. We couldn't communicate easily because / so I used my dictionary.

D Complete the conversation with *because* or *so.* Then practice it with a partner.

A: I'm stressed _____ we had a big test today.

B: How did you do?

A: Well, I didn't study, _____ I probably failed.

B: Why didn't you study?

A: I worked all day yesterday, _____ I didn't have time to study.

5 Writing An amazing experience

A Read the paragraphs below. Then, write about an amazing or unusual experience of your own.

> Last summer, I had the chance to go backpacking for ten days in Nepal. First, things were hard because I wasn't in shape and the air was thin. Every day, we hiked 16 kilometers. Sometimes I thought, "Am I going to survive?"
>
> After a few days, I was more comfortable. The scenery was very beautiful.
>
> The backpacking trip wasn't easy, but it was an amazing adventure!

B Exchange your writing with a partner. Ask your partner questions about his or her experience.

6 Communication Ten things to do

A Look at the activities below. Can you add one item to the list? Which things would you like to do? Check (✓) them. Which don't you want to do? Put an X next to them.

Ten things to do before you're 70

- ☐ learn to fly a plane
- ☐ live in another city
- ☐ start your own business
- ☐ learn to play an instrument (guitar, piano, etc.)
- ☐ gamble in Las Vegas or Monte Carlo
- ☐ get married
- ☐ drive an expensive car
- ☐ be on a reality TV show
- ☐ ride a camel in the desert
- ☐ Your idea: _____

B Get together with a partner. Ask and answer questions about your choices.

> I love flying, so I want to learn to fly a plane.

> Not me!

> Really? Why not?

> Because it's too scary!

 Check out the World Link video. Practice your English online at http://elt.heinle.com/worldlink

At the Movies

Lesson A   Now showing at a theater near you

1 Vocabulary Link   I'm a big fan of action films.

Look at the movie posters. Then read what each person has to say about movies. Ask and answer the questions with a partner.

 Notice!
We say: I like *action / classic / horror / science fiction* movies.

But: I like *musicals / romantic comedies.*

> Which movie(s) does each person want to see? not want to see?

> How do you know? Underline the words that tell you.

action

classic

musical

horror

science fiction

romantic comedy

ASK   ANSWER

What kind of movies do you like? Why? Can you name a movie that made you laugh? cry? feel good? think?

Derek

I'm not crazy about movies with a lot of singing and dancing. I like to see a lot of action.

Yee-un

Love stories are great. I like it when there's a happy ending. I also love old movies.

Khaliq

I'm not into serious documentaries. I prefer to see something that makes me laugh.

Isabel

I like scary movies. I'm also a big fan of movies about monsters and outer space.

2 Listening The movie is in 3-D.

A Look at the pictures. What are these people doing? Which word in the box describes each person?

bored   excited   talented

movie critic

movie actor

movie fan

CD 2
Track 32

B Listen to these three movie reviews. Who is speaking? Circle the correct picture in **A**. Then check the boxes.

Movie 1

☐ He liked it.

☐ He didn't like it.

Movie 2

☐ He liked it.

☐ He didn't like it.

Movie 3

☐ He liked it.

☐ He didn't like it.

CD 2
Track 33

C Listen. Which movie is being described? Match the movies (1, 2, or 3) to the sentences that describe them.

Movie 1

Movie 2

Movie 3

It was really boring.

It's good for children and their parents.

It has a happy ending.

It's in 3-D.

It's a horror movie.

It's a good movie to see with your boyfriend or girlfriend.

The music in the movie was good.

> **ASK ANSWER**
> Which movie sounds most interesting to you? Why?

3 Pronunciation Word stress to convey meaning

CD 2
Track 34

A Look at these pairs of sentences. Notice the underlined (stressed) words. Practice saying the sentences. Then listen and repeat.

1 a. It was <u>really</u> interesting.

2 a. No, it <u>starts</u> at eight thirty.

3 a. Yeah, I'm a <u>big</u> fan of scary movies.

4 a. It's a <u>romantic</u> <u>comedy</u>.

5 a. No, but the <u>ending</u> made me laugh.

b. It was really <u>interesting</u>.

b. No, it starts at eight <u>thirty</u>.

b. Yeah, I'm a big fan of <u>scary</u> movies.

b. It's a <u>romantic</u> comedy.

b. No, but the ending made me <u>laugh</u>.

CD 2
Track 35

B Listen to five questions. Circle the sentence above that is the best answer to each question.

4 Speaking   Can I take a message?

CD 2
Track 36

A Listen to the conversation. Take a phone message for Michael.

Pam: Hello?

Silvio: Hi. Is Michael there, please?

Pam: Who's calling?

Silvio: This is Silvio, a friend from school.

Pam: OK. Hang on a minute.

Silvio: Thanks.

Pam: Hello? Sorry. Michael's not here. Can I take a message?

Silvio: Yeah. We're going to a movie tonight. I have an extra ticket for Michael.

Pam: OK. What time does it start?

Silvio: In a half hour from now — at 8:00.

Pam: All right. I'll give him the message.

Silvio: Thanks a lot.

B Practice the conversation with a partner.

> **While You Were Out**
>
> Time of Call: _____
>
> _____ called.
> Movie is at _____ .
> He has _____
> for you.

ⓘ hang on = please wait

5 Speaking Strategy

A Write a movie you want to see, a time, a place, and a friend to invite.

Movie title	Time	Place	Friend's name

B With your partner, play one of these roles in a phone conversation. Use the Useful Expressions to help you.

> **Student A:** You call your friend to invite him or her to a movie. Your friend isn't home. Leave a message with a family member.
> **Student B:** Answer the phone. Take a message.

> Hello? Is Hiro there?

> **While You Were Out**
>
> Time of Call: _____
>
> Name of Caller: _____
>
> Message: _____
> _____
> _____

Useful Expressions
Telephoning
Hello? Is Michael there?
Who's calling, please?
This is Silvio.
OK. Hang on a minute.
Sorry. Michael's not home yet / not here.
Can I take a message?

C Switch roles and practice again.

6 Language Link *-ing / -ed* adjectives

A Read the sentences in the box. Pay attention to the adjectives in bold. Answer the questions.

> I'm **bored**. / This movie is **boring**. Let's watch something else.
>
> This work is **exhausting**. / I feel **exhausted**.

1. Which two words describe a person's emotion or feeling?

2. Which two words describe the cause of an emotion or feeling?

B Complete the movie review. Choose the correct form of the adjectives. Did Paula like the movie?

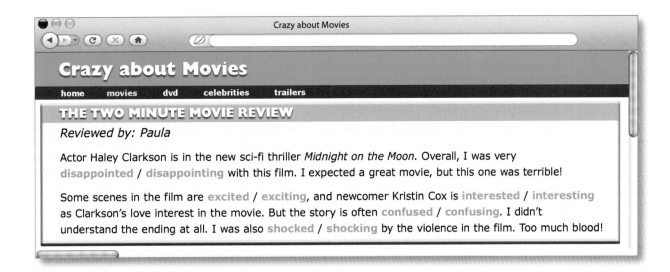

Crazy about Movies

Crazy about Movies

home   movies   dvd   celebrities   trailers

THE TWO MINUTE MOVIE REVIEW

Reviewed by: Paula

Actor Haley Clarkson is in the new sci-fi thriller *Midnight on the Moon*. Overall, I was very disappointed / disappointing with this film. I expected a great movie, but this one was terrible!

Some scenes in the film are excited / exciting, and newcomer Kristin Cox is interested / interesting as Clarkson's love interest in the movie. But the story is often confused / confusing. I didn't understand the ending at all. I was also shocked / shocking by the violence in the film. Too much blood!

C Complete these sentences. Use the correct form of the words in the box.

> confuse   depress   disappoint   embarrass   entertain   surprise   worry

1. He's two hours late. I'm getting _____.

2. I couldn't understand the movie. It was too _____.

3. My friend's sister had twins. I was _____ by the news.

4. That very _____ movie made me laugh a lot. I really enjoyed it.

5. My grandmother died last month, so I'm feeling a little _____.

6. I spilled coffee on my pants. How _____!

7. I was _____ because our team lost.

D Choose adjectives from **B** and **C** to complete the sentences. Then use the sentences to interview a partner.

1. Tell me about a(n) _____ experience you had.

2. When was the last time you were _____?

3. Talk about a(n) _____ movie you saw.

7 Communication   Movie reviews

A   What was the last movie you saw in a movie theater, online, on DVD, or on TV? Complete the chart with your information.

	Me	Partner 1	Partner 2
What was the last movie you saw?			
What type of film was it?			
Who was in the movie?			
Use two adjectives to describe the movie.			
Did you like the movie? Why or why not?			

B   Interview two classmates using the questions in **A**. Write their answers in the chart.

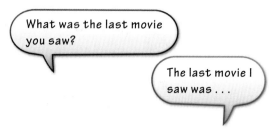

What was the last movie you saw?

The last movie I saw was . . .

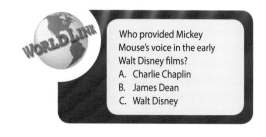

WORLD LINK

Who provided Mickey Mouse's voice in the early Walt Disney films?
A. Charlie Chaplin
B. James Dean
C. Walt Disney

C   Get into a group of two or three people you did not interview in **B**. Talk about the movies in your charts. Which one(s) do you want to see? Why?

I'd like to see . . . It sounds like an interesting movie.

At the Movies

Lesson B   On the set

1   Vocabulary Link   Be an extra!

Movie vs. *film*
We say: *movie* star,
movie theater
But: *film* festival
You can also use *film* as
a verb:
*We filmed the whole
movie indoors.*

A   Read about how you can appear in a movie. Complete the information with the verbs in the box.

| ask | bother | bring | include | make | see |

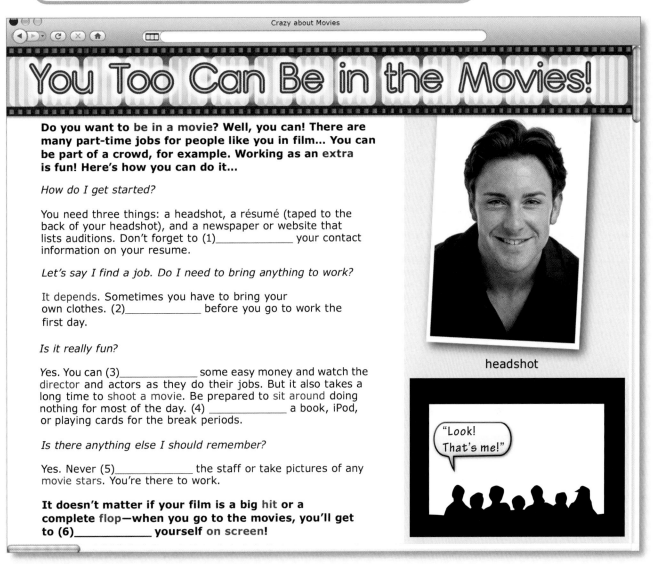

Crazy about Movies

You Too Can Be in the Movies!

Do you want to be in a movie? Well, you can! There are many part-time jobs for people like you in film... You can be part of a crowd, for example. Working as an extra is fun! Here's how you can do it...

How do I get started?

You need three things: a headshot, a résumé (taped to the back of your headshot), and a newspaper or website that lists auditions. Don't forget to (1)_____ your contact information on your resume.

Let's say I find a job. Do I need to bring anything to work?

It depends. Sometimes you have to bring your own clothes. (2)_____ before you go to work the first day.

Is it really fun?

Yes. You can (3)_____ some easy money and watch the director and actors as they do their jobs. But it also takes a long time to shoot a movie. Be prepared to sit around doing nothing for most of the day. (4) _____ a book, iPod, or playing cards for the break periods.

Is there anything else I should remember?

Yes. Never (5)_____ the staff or take pictures of any movie stars. You're there to work.

It doesn't matter if your film is a big hit or a complete flop—when you go to the movies, you'll get to (6)_____ yourself on screen!

headshot

"Look! That's me!"

B   Read the information in **A** again. Then answer the questions with a partner.

1. Look at the words in blue. Which ones refer to people who work in the movies? What do they do?

2. Which words refer to a successful or unsuccessful movie?

3. Would you like to be an extra in a movie? If so, what kind of film? If not, why not?

2 Listening   I'm in this movie.

A You are going to hear Melissa talk about working as an extra in a movie. Read the four sentences below. Which one(s) do you think she would say?

- ☐ The night before you work, sleep a lot.
- ☐ Eat a big meal in the morning before you leave.
- ☐ Wear something like shorts and a T-shirt to the job.
- ☐ Don't make any dinner plans on the day you work.

🔊 **CD 2 Track 37**

B Listen and check the pieces of advice in **A** Melissa would give.

🔊 **CD 2 Track 37**

C Listen again. Check *True* or *False*.

	True	False
1. Melissa and Diego are at the movies.	☐ True	☐ False
2. Melissa found the job in a newspaper.	☐ True	☐ False
3. She ate a lot of food at work.	☐ True	☐ False
4. She didn't sit very much.	☐ True	☐ False
5. She said "hello" to Nicole Fox.	☐ True	☐ False
6. The movie is a hit.	☐ True	☐ False

3 Reading   A remake

A Do you read movie reviews?
- ☐ always
- ☐ it depends
- ☐ never

WORLD LINK
In 1985, the movie *The Official Story* was the first South American film to win an Oscar. What country was the film from?
a. Chile
b. Argentina
c. Brazil

B Skim the two movie summaries on page 131 for 30 seconds. Then answer the question. What kind of movie is *Shutter*?
- a. ☐ a romantic comedy
- b. ☐ a horror film
- c. ☐ a documentary

SHUTTER (original)

In this hit from Thailand, Tun, a photographer, and his girlfriend, Jane, are driving home on a lonely country road one night. Suddenly, they see a girl in the road. Jane tries to stop the car, but it's too late. She hits and kills the girl. Feeling very afraid, Tun and Jane leave the girl and quickly drive back home to Bangkok.

Jane and Tun try to return to a normal life, but scary things start happening. Tun starts to have severe neck pain. And both Jane and Tun see scary shadows in Tun's photographs. The shadows look like a girl. Is it the girl on the road…?

SHUTTER (remake)

This movie was a remake[1] of a Thai movie with the same name. It was first released[2] in the United States and Canada. The critics thought it would flop, but it did well and made over $45 million worldwide.

The main characters are Jane and her husband, Ben. They move to Tokyo for Ben's new job. One night, they are in a car accident on a country road. They hit a young girl and drive into a tree. When they wake up, they look for the girl but they can't find her. Was the girl really there?

Jane and Ben try to forget the experience, but they can't. Then Ben's shoulder starts to hurt all the time. And when Ben develops his photos, there are strange lights in them. Ben's helper, Seiko, thinks the lights look like a girl. Is it the girl on the road . . . ?

[1] a remake = a new version of a film
[2] was released = was made available so that people could see it

---

C Read the sentences. Which movie does each one describe? Check "original," "remake," or both.

1. The woman's name is Jane. ☐ original ☐ remake
2. The man's name is Tun. ☐ original ☐ remake
3. There is a car accident. ☐ original ☐ remake
4. They see an image of the girl in photos. ☐ original ☐ remake
5. The story takes place in Japan. ☐ original ☐ remake
6. The man's neck hurts. ☐ original ☐ remake
7. The couple is married. ☐ original ☐ remake
8. The critics didn't like this movie. ☐ original ☐ remake

ASK ANSWER

Which famous movies shouldn't ever be remade? Why?

4 Language Link   The present continuous as future

A Read the sentences. Notice how the present continuous is used in each sentence. Then answer the questions with a partner.

> a. I'm seeing a movie with Ian tonight.
> b. After the movie, we're having dinner together.
> c. Eve is busy. She's watching a movie. Can you call back later?

 It is also possible to use *be going to* to talk about future plans:

I'm seeing a movie tonight.
I'm going to see a movie tonight.

1. Which sentence is about something happening now?_____

2. Which sentences are about future plans?_____

B Read the sentences. Underline the present continuous. Then write *N* for something happening now. Write *F* if the sentence talks about a future plan or activity.

1. Let's go! The movie <u>is starting</u> in twenty minutes. _____

2. I can't see a movie with you tonight. I'm meeting some friends at 8:00. _____

3. Nadia can't go to the movies, either. She's studying for a test in her room. _____

4. Are you meeting Carlos at the cafe later? _____

5. Why are you calling a cab? I can drive you to the theater now. _____

C Claudio is an actor. Follow these steps.

- Look at the photo. What is Claudio doing right now?

- Look at his upcoming schedule. With a partner, take turns making sentences about his plans. Use the present continuous.

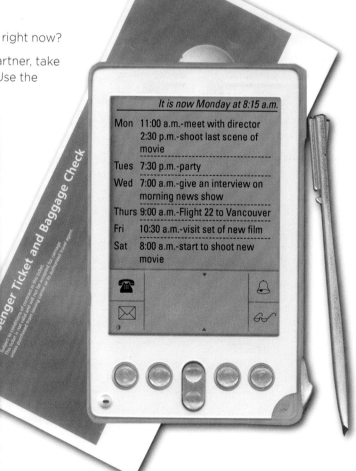

It is now Monday at 8:15 a.m.

Mon	11:00 a.m.-meet with director
	2:30 p.m.-shoot last scene of movie
Tues	7:30 p.m.-party
Wed	7:00 a.m.-give an interview on morning news show
Thurs	9:00 a.m.-Flight 22 to Vancouver
Fri	10:30 a.m.-visit set of new film
Sat	8:00 a.m.-start to shoot new movie

5 Writing **My favorite movie**

A Read the example. Then write about your favorite film of all time on a separate piece of paper.

> *My favorite movie of all time is Cinema Paradiso. It's a classic film—it was released in the 1980s. It's about a little Italian boy named Salvatore. He loves movies.*
>
> *In the film, Salvatore remembers his childhood. When he was young, he watched movies at the Cinema Paradiso, a movie theater in his hometown. He had an old friend named Alfredo. He fell in love with a girl named Elena.*
>
> *This is a very wonderful and romantic movie!*

B Exchange papers with a partner. What do you think of your partner's movie choice?

6 Communication **Better the second time?**

A Work with a partner. Read the directions to do this activity.

1. You and your partner work for a large movie studio. The studio wants to do a movie remake. Together, choose a movie to remake. It can be an old film, a new movie, or a foreign film.

   The movie we are going to remake: _____

   What kind of movie is it? _____

2. How are you going to remake the movie? Complete the chart with your ideas.

Who is going to star in the remake?	
When does the story in the movie take place (in the past, present, future)?	
How is the remake going to be different from the original?	
Are you going to give the remake a new title or use the original title?	

B Share your ideas with another pair. Listen to their ideas. Do you think your remakes are going to be successful? Why or why not?

 Check out the World Link video.   Practice your English online at http://elt.heinle.com/worldlink

Review: Units 10–12

1 Storyboard

A Leo and Emma are having lunch in the cafeteria. Look at the pictures and complete the conversations. More than one answer is possible for each blank.

1 Leo, can I _____? I want to call my friend, Eileen.

2 Your cell phone _____ _____! / Thanks! You can take pictures with it, too.

3 Hello. / Hi. ____ Eileen _____?

4 Sorry. She's _____. Can I _____? / No, thanks. I'll call her later.

5 Well, Eileen isn't home. Hey Leo, What's _____? / I _____. I think I ate too fast.

6 TEN MINUTES LATER... / I feel better. _____ _____ some dessert... / Leo! You're going to get sick!

B Practice the conversation with a partner. Then change roles and practice again.

2 See It and Say It

A Talk about the picture.

- Find these people in the picture:

  extras   actors   cameramen   director   movie star

- What's happening in the scene?

- Who looks surprised? bored? excited?

- What kind of movie is it?

B Get into a group of three or four people. You are going to perform the movie scene in the picture.

1. Discuss the scene. What's happening? Why do you think it's happening?

2. Choose a person in the scene to role play.

3. Create a short role play of six to eight sentences. Practice it with your group.

C Perform your scene for the class.

3 Times Change

A Look at the activities in the chart below. Add one more idea.

	Me		Partner 1		Partner 2	
	Now	5 years ago	Now	5 years ago	Now	5 years ago
drive						
speak a second language						
cook simple dishes						
your idea: _____						

B Ask your partners about the activities. Use *can* and *know how to* in your questions.

A: Can you drive?

B: Yes, I can. I passed the test last year.

A: Did you know how to drive five years ago?

B: No, I didn't. I was too young to drive.

C Look at the information in your chart. Which partner are you more similar to? Tell the class.

4 Listening

A Look at the pictures. Do these things ever happen where you live?

☐ how to survive a tornado   ☐ how to survive an earthquake   ☐ how to survive a house fire

B Listen. Tom is talking to a group of students. What are they talking about? Check (✔) the correct answer above.

CD 2
Track 38

C Listen again. Check (✔) the rules you should follow.

CD 2
Track 38

☐ Open the windows.

☐ Get under a desk.

☐ Go to the store for food and water.

☐ Don't stand near the windows.

☐ Go outdoors and stand in the street.

☐ Don't use matches.

D Have you ever been in an earthquake, a fire, a tornado, or a bad storm? Tell your partner what happened.

> Two years ago, there was a terrible storm in my hometown. It was scary. We couldn't leave the house . . .

5 Plans for the Day

A You are going to make an imaginary schedule for tomorrow. Write five activities from the box on the daily planner.

30 minutes	1 hour	1½ hours	2 hours
go grocery shopping get a haircut	go to the library do research on the internet	clean your apartment work out at the gym	do your homework meet a friend for coffee

10:00 am _____

10:30 am _____

11:00 am _____

11:30 am _____

12:00 pm _____

12:30 pm _____

1:00 pm _____

1:30 pm _____

2:00 pm _____

2:30 pm _____

3:00 pm _____

3:30 pm _____

4:00 pm _____

4:30 pm _____

5:00 pm _____

5:30 pm _____

6:00 pm _____

6:30 pm _____

7:00 pm _____

7:30 pm _____

8:00 pm _____

8:30 pm _____

B Think of a fun activity. Then invite your partner. Agree on a good time and write the activity on your daily planner.

A: What are you doing at 2:00 tomorrow?

B: I'm getting a haircut.

A: How about at 3:00?

B: Nothing. I'm free.

A: Great. Do you want to see a movie?

B: Sure, I'd love to!

C Think of a different fun activity and invite a new partner to join you.

Language Summaries

Unit 1 New Friends, New Faces

Lesson A

Vocabulary Link

cell (phone) number
city
e-mail address
first name
friends
hometown
interests
languages
last name
occupation

Speaking Strategy

Introducing yourself

My name is Mariana.
I'm Mariana.
 (It's) Nice to meet you.
 (It's) Nice to meet you, too.

Asking about occupations

What do you do?
 I'm a music student.

Lesson B

Vocabulary Link

Age
young
in her/his twenties
elderly (70 +)
Height
tall
average height
short
Weight
thin
slim
average weight
heavy-set
Eye color
blue
green

brown
dark
Hairstyle
long
short
straight
curly
spiky
Hair color
black
(light/dark)
 brown
blond
gray
red

Unit 2 Express Yourself!

Lesson A

Vocabulary Link

barking at
looking at
pointing at
shouting at
sitting on
smiling at
talking to
waving to

Additional Vocabulary

happy
sad
relaxed
nervous

Speaking Strategy

Greeting people and asking how they are

A: Hi, _____ . How's it going? /
Hi, _____ . How're you doing?
B: Fine. / OK. / All right. / Pretty
good. / Not bad. How about you?
A: I'm fine.

A: Hi, _____ . How's it going? /
Hi, _____ . How're you doing?
B: So-so. / Not so good.
A: Really? What's wrong?
B: I have a big test tomorrow.
I'm (a little) stressed. /
I'm (kind of) tired.

Lesson B

Vocabulary Link

angry
bored
cold
confident
confused

embarrassed
excited
hot
hungry
thirsty

Additional Vocabulary

call (someone)
cross one's fingers
point to something
shrug one's shoulders
shake hands

rushed
greeting
bow
kiss

Unit 3 What Do We Need?

Lesson A

Vocabulary Link

apple
banana
(loaf of) bread
butter
cake
(bunch of) carrots
(box of) cereal
cheese

chicken	orange juice
chips	(bag of) rice
eggs	salad
fish	(frozen) shrimp
French fries	soda
fresh	tofu
grapes	tomato
(ground) beef	yogurt

ice cream
(head of) lettuce
(carton of) milk
(instant) noodles

Additional Vocabulary

fast food
fresh food
frozen food
healthy food
junk food
organic food
prepared food

Speaking Strategy

Talking about things you need

Do we need any . . . ?
    Yes, we need . . .
    Yes, we do. We need . . .
    No, we don't. We (already)
        have . . . .
What else do we need?
    We still need . . .
    Nothing. I think we're all set.
Anything else?
    Yes, we need . . .
    No, that's it. We have everything.

Lesson B

Vocabulary Link

shop
coffee shop
gift / souvenir shop
to shop (online)

shopping
go shopping
grocery shopping
shopping bag
shopping cart
shopping mall /
    shopping center
window shopping

Additional Vocabulary

garage sale/yard sale
junk
spend money

Unit 4 Vacation!

Lesson A

Vocabulary Link

cloud/cloudy	hot
fog/foggy	warm
rain/rainy/raining	chilly
sun/sunny	cold
snow/snowy/	freezing
snowing	
wind/windy	

Additional Vocabulary

breezy
clear/(partly) cloudy skies
cool/warm temperatures
dry
heavy/light rain
strong/light winds

Speaking Strategy

Giving and Accepting/Refusing Advice (positive statement)

(I think) You should take a sweater.
    Good idea. / OK, I will.
    Really? I don't think so. /
    Really? I'd rather not.

Giving and Accepting/Refusing Advice (negative statement)

I don't think you should drive. /
You shouldn't drive.
    You're probably right.
    Really, I think I'll be OK.

Lesson B

Vocabulary Link

buy a plane ticket
check into your hotel
get a passport
go sightseeing
pack your suitcase
rent a car
show photos to friends
take photos
unpack

Additional Vocabulary

cash
credit card
identification

Unit 5 Heroes

Lesson A

Vocabulary Link

ambassador	doctor/
co-founder	physician
director	speechwriter
editor	teacher/
explorer	instructor
musician	teenager
politician	traveler/
researcher	tourist
speaker	writer

Additional Vocabulary

photographer	brave
journalist	documentary

Speaking Strategy

Agreeing with an opinion

Yeah, I agree./I know.
Yeah, you're right.

Follow-up question

What do you like about it?

Disagreeing with an opinion

Really? I don't think so.
Sorry, but I disagree.
I don't really agree.

Follow-up question

Why do you say that?

Lesson B

Vocabulary Link

look / looking
looking for
looking forward to
look up to
work
work as
work for (oneself)
work with
What kind of work do you do?
admire
find
be good at
hero
(night) shift

Unit 6 The Mind

Lesson A

Vocabulary Link

forget
forget to do (something)
never forget
will never forget
remember
can remember
good at remembering
   (something)
important to remember
have a bad/good memory

Speaking Strategy

Expressing degrees of certainty

Yes, they are./No, they aren't.
I think so./I don't think so.
Maybe./I'm not sure.
I have no idea.

Lesson B

Vocabulary Link

at noon/at midnight
be asleep/fall asleep
during the day/at night/
   in the middle of the night
go to bed (early)/stay up (late)
the day after tomorrow
the day before yesterday
wake up/get up
wake (someone) up

Unit 7 In the City

Lesson A

Vocabulary Link

ATM/cash machine
bookstore
cafe
gym/health club
hair salon

Lesson B

Vocabulary Link

polluted / pollution
a lot of pollution
not very polluted
pretty polluted

Unit 7 In the City (continued)

kiosk
movie theater
neighborhood
newsstand
train station

exercise
skip (breakfast)
work out

copy shop
grocery store
police station
nail salon
taxi stand
nightclub

Speaking Strategy

Asking about a specific place

Excuse me. Where's the Bridge Theater?
  It's on Jay Street.
  Go straight and turn left on Jay Street.
  It's in the middle of the block.

Asking about a place in general

Is there a gas station around here?
  Yes. Go one block. There's one on the corner of Court Street and First Avenue.

transportation
public transportation
affordable transportation
form of transportation
traffic
heavy/light traffic
traffic flow
stuck in traffic
rush hour
weather
pleasant weather
mild/severe weather
hot weather
humid weather
winters are . . .
summers are . . .

Unit 8 All About You

Lesson A

Vocabulary Link

play
badminton
baseball
basketball
ping-pong
soccer
tennis
video games
volleyball

go
bowling
camping
skiing
swimming

do
aerobics
Pilates
yoga
judo

Speaking Strategy

Inviting

Do you want to come?
  Sure, I'd love to!
  Sorry, I can't. I'm busy.
  Umm, no thanks. I'm not good at . . .

Offering

Do you want some ice cream?
  Yes, please. / Yes, thanks.
  No, thank you. / No, thanks. / I'm fine.

Lesson B

Vocabulary Link

ambitious/laid back
careful/careless
generous/selfish
organized/messy
talkative/reserved

bright
competitive
creative
impulsive
private

Additional Vocabulary

a little bit (+ *adj.*)
kind of (+ *adj.*)
somewhat (+ *adj.*)
possible/impossible
patient/impatient
perfect/imperfect

Unit 9 Change

Lesson A

Vocabulary Link

job
lose one's job/find a job
get a job
money
make more/less money
earn money
weight
lose/gain weight
shape
be in good/bad shape
be out of shape
smoking
start/stop smoking
quit smoking

Speaking Strategy

Making and responding to requests

Can/Could I borrow your cell phone?
Can/Could you lend me your cell phone?

Positive responses

Sure. No problem.
Certainly.

Negative response

I'm sorry but . . . . (+ *reason*)

Lesson B

Vocabulary Link

apply (for a job/to a university)
be about to (do something)
become (something)
can't take it (anymore)
get ready
take it easy
takes (time) to do (something)
take (time) off
take off (= depart)
take off (a piece of clothing)

Additional Vocabulary

join

Unit 10 Your Health

Lesson A

Vocabulary Link

arm	leg
back	muscle
bone	neck
chest	shoulder
foot	skin
hand	stomach
head	

Additional Vocabulary

broad	strong
long	backache
muscular	stomachache
narrow	sore throat
short	fever/
	temperature

Speaking Strategy

Talking about health problems

What's wrong? /
What's the matter?
  I don't feel well.
  I'm sick.
  I have a/an . . .
  My . . . hurts.

Lesson B

Vocabulary Link

energy
have (a lot of/more/less) energy
full of energy
low on energy
time
have time
give (someone) more time
stress
deal with stress, problems
(feel/be) stressed
reduce stress
stressful

under (a lot of) pressure
wait until the last minute

Additional Vocabulary

happy/unhappy
healthy/unhealthy
lucky/unlucky

Unit 11 That's Amazing!

Lesson A

Vocabulary Link

ability
lack the ability (to do something)
have a natural ability
talent
talented
have (got) lots of talent
talent show

be good at (something)
give up
get (millions of) hits
post videos

Speaking Strategy

Offering compliments and follow-up questions

Things

Nice haircut!
    Where did you get it done?
Cool glasses!
    Were they expensive?
This is/That's an interesting story.
    How long did it take to write it?
I like your jacket a lot.
    Is it new?
What a great painting!
    Was it difficult to do?

Abilities

You can speak English really well!
    How did you learn it so well?

Responses to compliments

Thanks!/Thank you.
That's nice of you to say.

Lesson B

Vocabulary Link

challenge
accept a challenge
chance
have a chance (to do something)
have a good chance (of doing something)
take the chance (to do something)
goal   **safe**
reach your goal   play it safe
risk
risk-taker   adventurous
risky   communicate
                  gambler

Additional Vocabulary

curious   harbor
dangerous   nutritious
famous   simple
frightening   tutor
(the) high point
    (of an experience)

Unit 12 At the Movies

Lesson A

Vocabulary Link

action (movie)
classic (movie)
horror (movie)
musical
romantic comedy
science fiction (movie)

be a big fan of (something)
be crazy about (something)
be into (something)
(happy/sad) ending
make (me/you) laugh/cry/
    feel good/think
scary

Speaking Strategy

Telephoning

Hello? Is Michael there?
    Who's calling, please?
This is Silvio.
    OK. Hang on a minute.
    Sorry. Michael's not home yet./
    Sorry. Michael's not here.
    Can I take a message?

Lesson B

Vocabulary Link

movie
be in a movie
shoot a movie
movie star
movie theater

film (n. and v.)
film festival

director
extra (n.)
flop/hit
it depends
on screen
sit around

Grammar Notes

Unit 1   New Friends, New Faces

Lesson A

Language Link: Review of the simple present

Yes/No questions with be	Positive responses	Negative responses
Are you a student?	Yes, I am.	No, I'm not.
Are they students?	Yes, they are.	No, they're not.* No, they aren't.
Is he a student?	Yes, he is.	No, he's not.* No, he isn't.

* In spoken English, this negative form is more common.

Yes/No questions with other verbs	Positive responses	Negative responses
Do you speak English?	Yes, I do.	No, I don't.
Does he speak Italian?	Yes, he does.	No, he doesn't.

Wh- questions				
Wh- word	Do/Does	Subject	Verb	
Where	do	you	live?	I live in London.
	does	she		She lives in Sao Paulo.
What	do	you	do on the weekend?	I go out with my friends.
	does	she		She spends time with her family.

Lesson B

Language Link: Describing people

What does he / she look like?	
Be + adjective	Have + (adjective) noun
Petra is young. She's in her teens. She's tall. She's thin.	Carlos has brown eyes. He has curly black hair. He has a beard and a mustache.

Unit 2 Express Yourself!

Lesson A

Language Link: Review of the present continuous

Positive statements

Subject	*Be*	Verb + *-ing*
I	am	
He/She	is	working.
You/We/They	are	

Contractions

I am = I'm
She is = She's
They are = They're

Negative statements

Subject	*Be*	*Not*	*Verb + ing*
I	am		
He/She	is	not	smiling.
You/We/They	are		

Contractions

I am not = I'm not
She is not = She's not*, She isn't
They are not = They're not*, They aren't

Yes/No questions and short answers

* More common in spoken English.

Be	Subject	Verb + *-ing*	Positive	Negative
Are	you they	**winning?**	Yes, I am. Yes, they are.	No, I'm not. No, they aren't.
Is	he/she		Yes, he/she is.	No, he/she isn't.

Wh- questions and answers

Wh- word	*Be*	Subject	Verb + *-ing*	
What	**are**	you	**doing?**	I'm reading.
	is	he/she		He's/She's talking on the phone.

Lesson B

Language Link: Object pronouns

In English, many sentences have a subject, a verb, and an object.

Subject Pronouns		Object Pronouns	
I	it	me	it
you	we	you	us
he	you (pl)	him	you
she	they	her	them

Subject	Verb	Object	
Carlos	knows	my parents.	• The object can be a noun or a pronoun.
He	likes	them.	• These verbs are followed by an object: *bring, buy, have, know, like, want.*

Unit 3 What Do We Need?

Lesson A

Language Link: Count / Noncount nouns with *some* and *any*

Count nouns		Noncount nouns
Singular	**Plural**	
a tomato	two tomatoes	bread, milk, sand, food
an orange	three oranges	

- Count nouns have singular and plural forms.
- Singular count nouns follow *a* or *an*.
- Plural count nouns can follow a number.
- Noncount nouns do not follow *a*, *an*, or a number. Noncount nouns are always singular.

Common Nouns	
Count	**Noncount**
a tomato	butter
an apple	fruit
a ring	jewelry
a job	work
a cup	tea
three desks	furniture
four dollars	money
two hours	time

Questions and short answers

	Question	**Positive**	**Negative**
Noncount nouns	Do we have **any** lettuce?	Yes, we have **some** (lettuce).	No, we don't have **any** (lettuce).
Plural count nouns	Do we have **any** potatoes?	Yes, we have **some** (potatoes). Yes, we have **three** (potatoes).	No, we don't have **any** (potatoes).

- Use *any* in questions and negative statements with noncount and plural count nouns.
- Use *some* in statements with noncount and plural count nouns.
- You can also answer these questions *Yes, we do,* and *No, we don't.*

Lesson B

Language Link: *Some / any, much / many, a lot of*

	Noncount nouns			Count nouns		
Positive	There's	a lot of some	clothing. jewelry.	There are	a lot of some	shoes. hats.
Negative	There isn't	much any	furniture. software.	There aren't	many any	books. toys.

Unit 4 Vacation!

Lesson A

Language Link: Connecting sentences with *but, or, so*

Connecting sentences, words, and phrases with *but, or, so*	
It's cold in Boston, **but** it's warm in Miami. It's cold **but** sunny in Vancouver today. It's a nice day **but** a little hot.	*But* shows an opposite idea or contrast. *But* joins words, phrases, and sentences.
We can go to the beach, **or** we can visit the zoo. Is it warm **or** chilly outside? Do you want coffee **or** tea?	*Or* gives a choice. *Or* joins words, phrases, and sentences.
It's raining, **so** we're not having a picnic in the park.	*So* gives a result. *So* joins sentences.

Lesson B

Language Link: *Whose;* possessive pronouns; *belong(s) to*

	Possessive adjectives	Possessive pronouns	Belong(s) to
Whose passport is this?	It's **my** passport. **your** **her** **his** **our** **their**	It's **mine.** **yours.** **hers.** **his.** **ours.** **theirs.**	It **belongs to me.** **you.** **her.** **him.** **us.** **them.**

- *Whose* and *who's* have the same pronunciation, but different meanings.
- *Whose* asks about the owner of something: Whose house is that? It's mine.
- *Who's* is a contraction of *Who* and *is*: Who's studying English? Maria is.

Unit 5 Heroes

Lesson A

Language Link: The past tense of *be*: statements and *yes / no* questions

Subject	*Be*		Past time expressions
I He/She	**was** **wasn't**	in Toronto	last year/summer. in 1984. twenty years ago.
You We They	**were** **weren't**		

Yes/No questions	**Were** you born in Mexico? **Yes, I was.** **No, I wasn't.** I was born in Chile.	**Was** Ms. Jones your teacher? **Yes, she was.** **No, she wasn't.**

Lesson B

Language Link: The simple past: regular verbs; *wh-* questions with *be*

The simple past: regular verbs		Common time expressions
I You He/She We They	visited didn't visit	Mexico last month.

- In the past tense, the verb form is the same for all persons.
- To form the negative, use *did not* or *didn't* + the base form of the verb.

The simple past tense of regular verbs: spelling rules

move -> moved	If the verb ends in *e*, add *d*.
visit -> visited	If the verb ends with a consonant, add *ed*.
study -> studied	If the verb ends in consonant + *y*, change the *y* to *i* and add *ed*.
play -> played	If the verb ends with vowel + *y*, add *ed*.
stop -> stopped	With one-syllable verbs that end with a consonant-vowel-consonant, double the last letter and add *ed*.
fix -> fixed	But . . . do not double the last consonant if it is a *w* or *x*.
occur -> occurred	With two-syllable verbs that end with a consonant-vowel-consonant, double the last consonant if the last syllable is stressed.
listen -> listened	But . . . do not double the last consonant if the last syllable is not stressed.

Wh- questions with *be*	Answers
Who was Alyssa?	(She was) Alec's classmate.
Why was Alec shy?	(Because) he liked Alyssa.
When was their date?	(It was) on the weekend.
Where was their date?	(It was) at a restaurant.
What was in the waiter's hand?	A twenty-dollar bill.

Unit 6 The Mind

Lesson A

Language Link: The simple past: irregular verbs

The simple past: irregular verbs		
I You He/She We They	forgot the tickets at home. didn't forget the tickets at home.	Do not add *-ed* to irregular past tense verbs in affirmative statements. See the list of irregular verbs on page 149. To form the negative, use *did not* or *didn't* + the base form of the verb.

Base form	Past tense	Base form	Past tense	Base form	Past tense
begin	began	feel	felt	run	ran
bring	brought	forget	forgot	say	said
buy	bought	get	got	shake	shook
come	came	give	gave	speak	spoke
do	did	go	went	take	took
drink	drank	have	had	teach	taught
eat	ate	know	knew	think	thought
fall	fell	make	made	win	won

Lesson B

Language Link: The simple past: question forms

	Yes/No questions	Answers
Regular verbs	Did you study for the test?	Yes, I did. No, I didn't.
Irregular verbs	Did you forget the tickets?	Yes, I did. No, I didn't.

	Wh- questions	Answers
Regular verbs	When did you study?	(I studied) last night.
Irregular verbs	Where did you forget the tickets?	(I forgot them) at home.

Unit 7   In the City

Lesson A

Language Link: Prepositions of place

Prepositions of place	at, on, and in
The library is **across from** Jimmy's Gym. The subway is **next to** Carl's Cafe. The bus stop is **in front of** the Bridge Theater. The bank is **behind** Pat's Hair Salon. The bookstore is on Second Avenue, **between** Court Street and Jay Street.	at + building: **at** the mall; **at** the office at + address: It's **at** 226 Spear Street. on + street: It's **on** Spear Street. on + floor: It's **on** the third floor. in + room: **in** her room; **in** the kitchen NOTE: in bed, in class, at school, at home

Lesson B

Language Link: Questions and answers with *How much / How many*

How many is used with count nouns	*How much* is used with noncount nouns

How many parks are there?
    There are **a lot.** / **A lot.**
    There are **a few.** / **A few.**
    There are **two.** / **Two.**
    There are**n't many.** / **Not many.**
    There are**n't any.** / **None.**
	How much pollution is there?
	    There's **a lot.** / **A lot.**
	    There's a **little.** / **A little.**
	———
	    There is**n't much.** / **Not much.**
	    There is**n't any.** / **None.**

Unit 8 All About You

Lesson A

Language Link: Verb + noun; verb + infinitive

Verb + noun	
I love/like/hate/enjoy **sports**.	A **noun** or **noun phrase** can follow many verbs.
Verb + infinitive	
I love/like/learned **to play tennis**. I want/plan **to visit Australia** next year.	The **infinitive** is *to* + the base form of a verb. The **infinitive** can follow certain verbs. Some of these are *like, love, hate, want, plan,* and *expect.*

Lesson B

Language Link: How often . . . ?; frequency expressions

How often do you check email?	**Every** **Every other**	day/Monday/week/ month/year/summer.
How often do you see your grandparents?	**Once/Twice/Three times** **Several times**	a day/a week/a month/ a year.
How often do you text your friends?	**All the time.** (= very often) **Once in a while.** (= sometimes) **Hardly ever.** (= almost never)	

- *How often* asks about the frequency of an event.
- Don't use *How often* with the present continuous.
- Expressions of frequency (*every day, once in a while*) usually come at the end of a sentence. Sometimes they come at the beginning.

Unit 9 Change

Lesson A

Language Link: *Like to* vs. *Would like to*

Do	Subject	*Like*	Infinitive	
	I	like	to visit	Australia. My favorite place is Bondi Beach.
Do	you			Australia?
- Use *like* + infinitive to ask a question or state a fact about the *present*.				

Would	Subject + would	Like	Infinitive	
	I'd			Australia next year.
Would	you	like	to visit	Australia?

- Use *would like* + infinitive to ask a question or state a *future* hope or desire.

Contractions

I'd = I would
you'd = you would
he'd = he would
she'd = she would
we'd = we would
they'd = they would

Lesson B

Language Link: The future with *be going to*

Subject + *be*	(Not)	Going to	Verb		Future time expressions
I'm You're He's/She's We're They're	(not)	going to	visit	Mexico	tomorrow. this summer. next month/year/summer. after graduation.

- Use *be going to* to talk about future plans: I'm going to visit Mexico next month.
- Use *be going to* to make predictions: Don't worry. You're going to do great on the test!
- *Going to* is often said as "gonna." Don't use "gonna" in writing.

Contractions

I'm = I am
you're = you are
he's = he is
she's = she is
we're = we are
they're = they are

Yes/No questions	Are you going to visit Mexico this summer? Yes, I am./Yes, maybe./No, I'm not.
Wh- questions	What are you going to do this summer? I'm going to visit Mexico.

Unit 10 Your Health

Lesson A

Language Link: The imperatives; unit nouns

Positive imperatives

Base form	
Relax	for a while. You're tired.
Take	your medicine twice a day.
Go	two blocks and turn left.
Be	quiet!

Negative imperatives

Don't	Base form	
Don't	smoke	in here.
Don't	travel	without your passport.

- Use the imperative to give advice, instructions, directions, and orders.
- Also use the imperative to make requests. Add *please* to make orders and requests more polite: Please be quiet! Don't smoke in here, please.

Noncount nouns	Count nouns
Do you like <u>soup</u>?	I'd like **a cup of** <u>soup</u>, please.
I only have <u>cake</u> on special occasions.	I'm going to eat **that piece of** <u>cake</u> in the refrigerator.
There was <u>water</u> everywhere.	Is this **your glass of** <u>water</u>?
Do you prefer <u>bread</u> or rice?	Can you pick up **a loaf of** <u>bread</u> at the store?
You can't wear <u>jeans</u> to the party.	I bought a shirt and **two pairs of** <u>jeans</u>.

Use expressions like *a cup of* and *a piece of* to make noncount nouns "countable."

Lesson B

Language Link: *When* clauses

When clause	Result clause
When(ever) I drink a lot of coffee,	I can't sleep.
When(ever) I see sad movies,	I cry.

- These sentences talk about things that are usually true: When X happens, Y is the result.
- In the *when* clause, you can also use the word *whenever*.
- The present tense is used in the *when* clause and in the result clause.

Result clause	*When* clause
I can't sleep	when(ever) I drink a lot of coffee.

- The result can come first in a sentence. In this case, there is no comma between the result and the *when* clause.

Unit 11 That's Amazing!

Lesson A

Language Link: Talking about talents with *can* and *know how to*

Present	Past
Naoki can play the guitar.	Monika could read at age two.
can't	couldn't
Naoki knows how to play the guitar.	Monika knew how to read at age two.
doesn't know how to	didn't know how to

- Use *can* and *know how to* to talk about abilities you learn:
  I can speak some Chinese, but I don't know how to read it.
- Do not use *know how to* for inherent abilities:
  Correct: I can't see without my glasses. Incorrect: ~~I don't know how to see without my glasses.~~

Lesson B

Language Link: Connecting ideas with *because* and *so*

Main clause	Reason clause
I'm hungry	**because** I didn't eat breakfast.

- *Because* joins two sentences together. It comes at the beginning of the reason clause.
- *Because* answers the question *why*—it gives a reason.
- To answer questions in conversation, people often give the reason only. Please note that this style is not correct for formal, written English: Why are you hungry? <u>Because</u> I didn't eat breakfast.

Reason clause	Main clause
Because I didn't eat breakfast,	I'm hungry.

- When the reason comes first, put a comma between the reason and the main clause.

Main clause	Result clause
I was hungry,	**so** I ate lunch.

- *So* joins two sentences together. It comes at the beginning of a result clause.
- *So* answers the question what did you do—it gives a result.

Unit 12   At the Movies

Lesson A

Language Link: *-ing* / *-ed* adjectives

-ed adjectives	*-ing* adjectives
What subjects are you interested in? When she gets bored in class, she falls asleep. He felt embarrassed because he tore his jeans.	That movie is really interesting. Math class is so boring. What is your most embarrassing memory?

- *-ed* adjectives describe a person's feeling.
- *-ing* adjectives describe the cause of a feeling.

Lesson B

Language Link: The present continuous as future

Subject + *be*	Verb + *-ing*		Use the present continuous to talk about:
She's	sleeping	right now. Can you call back later?	• actions happening now
I'm	studying	at UCLA this summer.	• actions happening "these days"
We're	seeing	a movie tonight at 7:00.	• future plans

- It's possible to use the present continuous or *be going to* to talk about future plans: We're seeing/going to see a movie tonight at 7:00.
- We do not use the present progressive with *stative* verbs, for example: *be, love, hate, (dis)like, want, need, know, think, have.*

Answer Key

Answers to **page 89**, Communication: Personality Quiz, **Activity B**

Green	Blue	Purple	Orange
You're generous and you care about other people. You want to help them. But sometimes, you're too picky! Remember, people aren't perfect.	You're ambitious and a little bit reserved. But remember—it's important to smile. Don't be so serious all the time!	You love to learn and try new things. You're also very bright. But sometimes, you're too competitive. Let others win once in a while!	You're interesting, and you love adventure. But be careful! Sometimes you're very impulsive! Remember to think about your future, too!